CW01403523

# LUKE MANGAN CLASSICS

Luke Mangan is one of Australia's best-known and most talented chefs. He has opened three restaurants in Sydney to great acclaim: Salt (which won two chef's hats) Bistro Lulu and Moorish. In 2004 he was invited to cook for the wedding festivities of Crown Prince Frederick and Mary Donaldson in Denmark.

Hardie Grant Books

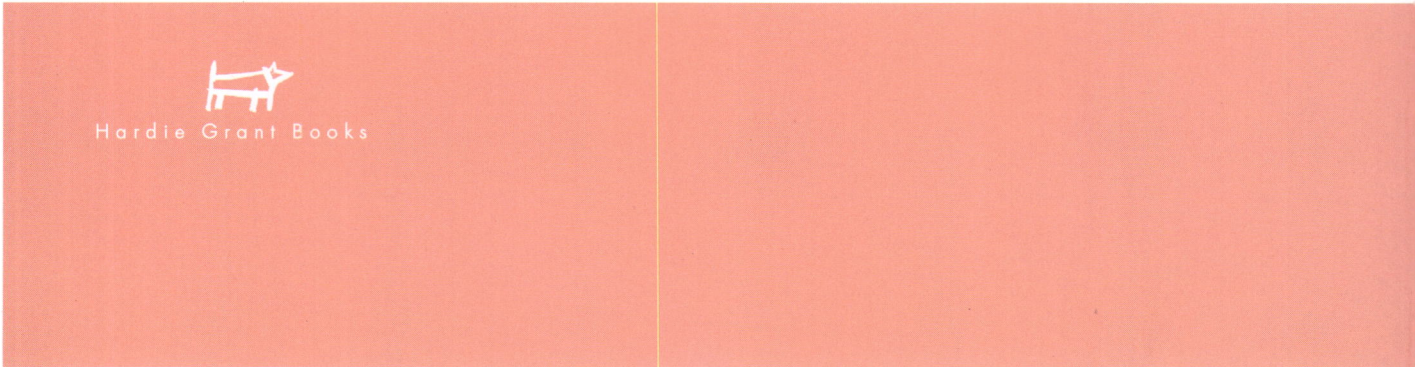

# LUKE
# MANGAN
# CLASSICS

*To Lucy Allon*
*My business partner, and the person without whose trust in me*
*none of this would be where it is today.*

Published in 2005
by Hardie Grant Books
85 High Street
Prahran, Victoria 3181, Australia

www.hardiegrant.com.au

All rights reserved. No part of this publication may be reproduced, stored in a retrieval system or transmitted in any form by any means, electronic, mechanical, photocopying, recording or otherwise, without the prior written permission of the publishers and copyright holders.

The moral right of the author has been asserted.

Text © Luke Mangan 2005 (see note on recipes below)

Photography © Adrian Lander 2000, 2005 and Anson Smart 2002, 2005

**Recipes** on pages 5, 6, 9, 16, 17, 20, 21, 24, 27, 29, 32, 34, 42, 46, 50, 51, 52, 56, 59, 62, 64, 65, 66, 72, 73, 78, 80, 82, 84, 86, 87, 88, 90, 91, 93, 96, 97, 100, 101, 102, 110, 112, 113, 114, 116, 118, 122, 128, 129, 130, 133, 137, 139, 144, 150, 154, 157, 160, 161, 164, 168, 172, 176, 178, 179, 180, 182, 184, 185, 186, 188, 189, 192, 194, 196, 200, 206, 208, 212, 213, 214, 218, 219, 221, 222, 223, 224 © **Lisa Hudson** and **Luke Mangan** 2000, 2005

National Library of Australia Cataloguing-in-Publication Data:

A catalogue record for this book is available from the National Library of Australia.

**Design** by **Trisha Garner**

**Photography** on pages 4, 7, 25, 28, 35, 43, 47, 53, 57, 67, 81, 85, 89, 103, 111, 115, 119, 131, 151, 155, 165, 173, 181, 187, 195, 207, 209, 215, 222, 224 by **Adrian Lander**

**Photography** on pages 3, 11, 15, 18, 23, 31, 38, 41, 61, 71, 75, 77, 95, 98, 127, 135, 141, 147, 159, 163, 167, 171, 177, 191, 199, 203, 211 by **Anson Smart**

Printed and bound by Imago

10  9  8  7  6  5  4  3  2  1

# Contents

# Starters & Soups

# Pea Shooter

20 g (⅔ oz) butter

½ onion, peeled and chopped

125 ml (4 fl oz) white wine

350 g (12 oz) frozen peas

1 bunch (125 g/4 oz) English spinach, washed and stems removed

100 ml (3½ fl oz) cream

sea salt

1 lemon

Melt butter and gently soften the onion until translucent. Add white wine and allow to bubble until liquid has reduced considerably, then add peas, cover with boiling water and bring back up to the boil. Take off the heat immediately and strain peas and onion mix, retaining liquid. Add spinach to hot peas, so spinach wilts, then add ice to the vegetables to refresh and cool them quickly.

Blend vegetable mix, slowly adding reserved liquid, until purée reaches the consistency of soup. Semi-whip cream and fold three-quarters of it through the soup, plus a pinch of salt and the juice of half the lemon (taste for acidity).

*Serves 4–6*

**To serve** Serve pea soup cold in shot glasses (2 per person) with a tiny dollop of cream on top.

**Notes** Other vegetables can be used: cauliflower, pumpkin or potato and leek would all taste good.

The vegetables must be cooled quickly or the soup will be a muddy colour, not bright green.

# Beetroot Soup with Horseradish

2 medium–large beetroot

1 tbsp butter

1 tbsp extra-virgin olive oil

25 ml (1 fl oz) sherry vinegar

1 tsp horseradish relish,
plus extra for serving

sea salt and freshly ground
black pepper

Peel the beetroot and slice into pieces about 5 mm wide (¼ in). Heat the butter and extra-virgin olive oil in a heavy-based saucepan, add the beetroot and toss to coat in the oil and butter. Cook, covered, on a very low heat for about 1 hour. Keep checking to make sure it doesn't catch and burn.

Add the vinegar and *just* cover the beetroot with water and cook for a further 20 minutes. Remove from heat (do not drain), add the horseradish and purée in a food processor until it is very smooth. You will need to add 100 ml (3½ fl oz) to achieve the desired consistency. Season to taste. Refrigerate.

*To serve* Serve the soup well chilled in shot glasses, with a tiny dollop of horseradish relish on top.

# Freshly Shucked Oysters with Wasabi, Soy & Leek Dressing

24 oysters, freshly shucked

3 leeks, white part only

4 sheets nori (seaweed)

1 lemon, quartered

**Dressing**

1 tube (about 40 g/1½ oz) prepared wasabi (Japanese horseradish)

1 tsp sesame oil

1 tbsp soy sauce

1 tbsp hot water

150 ml (5 fl oz) extra-virgin olive oil

**For the dressing** Whisk together the wasabi, sesame oil, soy sauce and water, then gradually pour in the extra-virgin olive oil, whisking continuously until well incorporated.

**For the leeks** Cut the leeks in half vertically, then in half vertically again, then in half horizontally, to create small batons. Bring some salted water to the boil and blanch the leeks for a couple of minutes. Drain. Mix the leeks with half the dressing.

*Serves 4*

**To serve** *Place some ice on a large shallow dish. Sprinkle with salt (this helps prevent the ice melting too quickly). Arrange the oysters in their shells on the ice, top with leeks and drizzle with remaining dressing. Garnish with roughly torn nori and lemon wedges.*

# Coconut Broth with Yabbies & Lime

1–1.5 litres (1⅔–2½ pt) fish stock
(see page 219)

12 yabbies

1 lime

50 ml (1⅔ fl oz) water

50 g (1¾ oz) sugar

**Broth**

50 g (1¾ oz) butter

100 g (3½ oz) shallots,
peeled and halved

50 g (1¾ oz) fish trimmings, flesh only

400 ml (13 fl oz) fish stock
(see page 219)

400 ml (13 fl oz) coconut milk

100 g (3½ oz) coconut milk powder

1 kaffir lime leaf

**Spice mix**

1 tsp chilli flakes

1 tsp ground ginger

1 tsp garlic powder

1 tsp coriander seeds, ground

1 tsp ground lemon myrtle

**To make the broth** Melt butter in a pot and add shallots and fish trimmings and cook on low heat to seal without colouring. Add fish stock, coconut milk and powder, and the lime leaf and bring to the boil. Simmer for 10 minutes, remove from the heat and leave stock to infuse for 1 hour. Blend and then strain through a fine strainer and set aside.

**For the yabbies** Bring a saucepan of fish stock to the boil, put yabbies in for approximately 3 minutes or until the shells are pink. Plunge yabbies into iced water to refresh. Peel and discard everything except the tail. Keep refrigerated until ready to use.

Peel the skin off the lime and, using a sharp knife, remove the white pith and discard. Julienne the skin. Blanch in a little bit of boiling water, to remove any bitter taste. Juice the lime. Mix together water, sugar, lime juice and lime zest and boil in a small pan until sugar dissolves.

**For the spice mix** Combine spices together.

*Serves 4*

**To serve** *Reheat the broth and lightly poach the yabbies until warm, but be careful not to overcook. Place a quarter of the ground spice mix in the middle of each bowl, and place 3 yabbies on top with a ladleful of broth. Garnish with lime zest and syrup.*

**Note** *In addition to the lime you can garnish with chopped coriander also.*

# Carrot Broth with Spices

1 tsp extra-virgin olive oil

4 shallots, finely sliced

1 tbsp butter

2 tbsp curry spice blend (buy
a good one or make up your
own using your choice of
ground chilli, cumin, coriander,
turmeric, paprika, fenugreek)

sea salt and freshly ground
black pepper

800 ml (1 pint 10 fl oz) freshly
squeezed carrot juice

Heat the extra-virgin olive oil and
add the shallots. Cook until crisp,
then drain on paper towel. Set aside.

Melt the butter in a large saucepan over
medium heat. Add the curry spices
and season. Pour on the carrot juice
and bring to the boil. Remove from the
stove and using a hand-held blender
froth the soup for a few seconds.

*Serves 4*

*To serve* Pour broth into serving
*bowls and garnish with the shallots.*

# Cauliflower Soup

40 g (1½ oz) butter

2 onions, finely sliced

2 medium-sized cauliflowers,
roughly chopped

1 litre (2 pints) milk

sea salt and freshly ground
black pepper

60 ml (2 fl oz) cream

½ bunch chives, finely chopped

truffle oil (optional)

Melt the butter in a large saucepan.
Add the onion and cook over a gentle
heat until soft, making sure it does
not go brown. Add the cauliflower
to the pan and cook, stirring
occasionally, for about 5 minutes.

Pour in enough milk to just cover
the vegetables ( you may not need
the whole litre), bring to the boil
and simmer for 20–30 minutes,
or until the cauliflower is soft.

In a blender, purée the cauliflower
mixture until smooth, then pass
through a fine sieve if you want
to make it velvety smooth (this is
optional). Return to the saucepan,
season, then add the cream
and bring to the boil again.

*Serves 6*

*To serve* Drizzle with a little truffle
*oil and sprinkle with chives.*

# Garlic & Rosemary Pizzas

**Base**

500 g (1 lb) plain flour

1 tsp sea salt

7 g dried yeast (1 sachet)

250 ml (1 cup) lukewarm water

**Topping**

1 head garlic

½ bunch (about 45 g/1½ oz) rosemary

100 g (3½ oz) grated parmesan

sea salt and freshly ground
black pepper

½ bunch rocket (about 2 handfuls)

juice of 2 lemons

extra-virgin olive oil

Preheat oven to 170°C (340°F).
Cut the tip off the garlic and
drizzle with olive oil, wrap up in
foil and roast in oven for an hour,
or until soft. Squeeze garlic out of
skins and reserve until needed.

**For pizza base** Put flour in a bowl
with salt and make a well in its centre.
Dissolve yeast in the water, stirring
with a fork and pour into well. Slowly
incorporate water and flour then, when
a ball, remove from bowl and knead on
a floured bench for at least 15 minutes
or until smooth (alternatively, use the
bread hook of a mixer). Let dough
stand for approximately 30 minutes.

Pick leaves of rosemary from
stems. Blanch half the leaves, and
chop the rest. Wash rocket and
remove any chunky stems. Increase
oven heat to 220°C (425°F).

**To make the pizza** Roll dough into
6 balls. Roll these out flat with a
rolling pin until the base is 3–4 mm
(¼ in) thick. Spread roasted garlic on
the base, sprinkle with blanched sprigs
and chopped rosemary, then parmesan
on top and season with salt and pepper.
Put on a greased oven tray and cook
until golden brown – approximately
5–10 minutes, but check constantly
to ensure they are not overcooking.

Dress rocket with lemon juice and
olive oil and scatter over the top.

*Serves 6*

*To serve* Cut each pizza into
quarters and pile up on a platter,
or serve individually on plates
garnished with extra rocket.

# Cream of Asparagus Soup

4 bunches (about 1 kg/2 lb) asparagus

2 onions

1 bunch (120 g/4 oz) English spinach

2 potatoes

60 g (2 oz) butter

250 ml (1 cup) water

500 ml (2 cups) cream

sea salt

Chop tips from asparagus and set aside. Trim asparagus stalks. Peel and roughly chop onions. Thoroughly wash the spinach and drain. Peel and dice the potato into 2 cm (¾ in) cubes.

Melt butter in a large pan and cook the onion slowly – sweat it – until translucent. Add asparagus stalks, potato and water. Cover pan with lid and cook until vegetables are semi-soft, then add more water until vegetables are covered, bring to the boil with lid off and simmer gently until potato is soft.

Remove pan from the heat, add spinach and stir through. Strain off the liquid and chill the vegetable mix with sufficient ice to stop it discolouring. When cool, blend vegetable mix, slowly adding cream as you process, and season with salt to taste.

*Serves 4–6*

**To serve** Heat soup in a pan and when boiling add the asparagus tips. Continue to cook for a few minutes then ladle into your favourite bowl.

**Notes** It is very important to add ice to the cooked vegetables to stop them cooking otherwise the whole soup will be brown.

In winter put the soup bowls in the oven for a few minutes to take the chill off them before ladling in soup, and serve with a crusty loaf of bread.

You can use the same simple method to make soup with other vegetables, for example cauliflower, broccoli and bacon – add fried bacon as a garnish at the end.

# Asparagus with Smoked Salmon Dip

200 g (7 oz) smoked salmon

2 tbsp sour cream

150 ml (5 fl oz) cream

juice of 1 lemon

1 tsp cayenne pepper

1 tsp paprika

4 bunches asparagus (about 1 kg/2 lb)

Blend smoked salmon in the food processor or chop it finely with a sharp knife. Mix salmon with the sour cream then slowly add the rest of the cream. Season with lemon juice, cayenne and paprika.

Hold the bottom and the middle of each asparagus spear and snap (it will snap where it is not woody), then blanch in boiling, salted water for 1 minute and refresh in iced water.

*Serves 4–6*

*To serve* Divide asparagus and salmon dip between plates.

# Prawns with Dill Mayonnaise

12 large cooked prawns

1 cup diced mango

sea salt and freshly ground black pepper

handful of dill sprigs

toasted sourdough bread or Melba toast

**Mayonnaise**

2 free-range egg yolks

2 tsp Dijon mustard

2 tsp white wine vinegar

200 ml (7 fl oz) extra-virgin olive oil

4 tbsp chopped dill

To make the mayonnaise, place the yolks, mustard and vinegar in a bowl and whisk until all combined. Slowly whisk in olive oil until the mixture forms mayonnaise consistency. Stir through dill.

Peel and de-vein the prawns. Chop roughly. Combine the prawns, mango and mayonnaise and season to taste.

*Serves 4*

*To serve* Divide between plates garnished with extra dill sprigs and offer toast.

# Scallop & Chive Dumplings

200 g (7 oz) cod (blue-eye or
other firm white fish)

300 g (10½ oz) rock salt

600 ml (20 fl oz) milk

1 small onion, peeled and quartered

2 cloves garlic

4 bay leaves

300 g (10½ oz) mashed potato
(see page 166)

130 g (4 oz) scallops

1 bunch chives, finely chopped

nutmeg for grating

sea salt (optional)

1 packet round gow gee wrappers

Cover cod liberally with rock salt, leave for 30 minutes in the fridge and then rinse.

Heat milk with onion, garlic cloves and bay leaves until simmering. Skim the froth off the milk, place cod in the milk and simmer gently so the surface just ticks over, for approximately 8 minutes or until fish is cooked. Strain and keep poaching liquor but discard vegetables and bay. Blend fish with a little liquor and then pass through a sieve to make a cod purée.

Heat mash until warm and add to cod purée, then add sufficient poaching liquor to bring the consistency to that of a soft dough. Set aside to cool. Roughly dice the scallops and chop the chives and add to the fish mix when it is cool. Add a pinch of freshly grated nutmeg and a pinch of salt if you think it needs it.

Lay out wrappers on the bench and place 1 heaped teaspoon of mix in the centre of each wrapper, brush the edges with a little water using a pastry brush and fold edges together in the centre, making sure the wrap is sealed well. Steam for 4 minutes and serve warm.

*Serves 4–6*

**Notes** *For a very elegant touch, blanch some long chives quickly then refresh them in cold water and tie around the top of the dumplings.*

*Dumplings can also be cooked quickly in boiling water or deep fried, but you should then use beaten egg to seal them and let them rest in the fridge before cooking.*

*Gow gee wrappers can be purchased from an oriental grocer and can be stored in the freezer before being defrosted and then kept in the refrigerator for use.*

# Mussels in Curry Dressing with Hot Mint

2 tbsp curry powder (buy a good blend or make up your own e.g. ground chilli, cumin, coriander, turmeric, fenugreek)

3 tbsp red wine vinegar

120 ml (4 oz) extra-virgin olive oil

2 bunches Vietnamese mint

30 g (1 oz) butter

2 onions, sliced

1½ kg (3 lb) mussels, scrubbed clean and beards removed

200 ml (6½ fl oz) dry white wine

**For the dressing** Roast the curry powder by sprinkling it into a small saucepan and cooking it over low heat until fragrant. Pour in the vinegar then whisk in the extra-virgin olive oil. Season and set aside.

**For the garnish** Remove the leaves of one bunch of Vietnamese mint (keep the stalks) and chop finely. Set aside.

**For the mussels** In a large saucepan, heat the butter. Add the onions and cook until soft, then add the mussels (discard any that have opened before cooking), the other bunch of Vietnamese mint plus the mint stalks. Cover with a lid and cook for 5 minutes. Add the white wine, put the lid on again and cook for a further few minutes. Lift the lid to check whether the mussels have opened. If they have, remove them, and place in deep serving bowls. Keep cooking with the lid on until all the mussels have opened (discard any that do not open).

*Serves 4*

*To serve* When all the mussels are in bowls, strain the pan juices, spoon plenty over the mussels, drizzle with curry dressing and sprinkle with chopped mint.

*Serve with crusty bread to mop up the juices.*

# Salmon Rillette

250 g (8 oz) salmon fillets

splash of white wine

pinch of mixed herbs

150 ml (5 fl oz) mayonnaise
(see page 223)

2 tbsp finely chopped dill

1 tsp finely chopped chives

sea salt and freshly ground
black pepper

40 g (1½ oz) mixed salad greens,
lightly dressed in vinaigrette

12 cornichons

4 slices brioche or sourdough bread

extra-virgin olive oil

**For the salmon** Remove any bones from the salmon. In a shallow pan, gently poach the salmon in water with a splash of white wine and herbs, to medium-rare (about 5 minutes). Remove from the pan and place in a large bowl.

**For the rillette** Using a fork, roughly flake the poached salmon, then fold in the mayonnaise, dill and chives. Season well.

*Serves 4*

**To serve** *Spoon the rillette onto each plate in a neat mound. Place a small pile of salad next to the rillette and 3 cornichons next to that. Toast the bread, slice in half on the diagonal and place on the plates. Drizzle extra-virgin olive oil over and around the rillette.*

# Tuna with Wasabi Dressing

2 tsp wasabi

1 tsp sesame oil

1 tbsp soy sauce

1 tbsp hot water

150 ml (5 fl oz) extra-virgin olive oil

400 g (14 oz) sashimi-quality tuna

50 g (1¾ oz) ginger

3 shallots

Slowly mix wasabi, sesame oil, soy sauce and hot water together. Then slowly whisk in olive oil.

Cut the tuna into 1 cm (⅓ in) thick slices and sear in a hot pan for a few seconds on each side.

Peel and julienne ginger; peel and thinly slice shallots. Shallow fry shallots until golden brown. Drain.

*Serves 4–6*

**To serve** *Divide tuna slices between plates and sprinkle ginger and shallots on top. Drizzle the dressing over.*

**Notes** *You can ask your fishmonger to slice the tuna for you.*

*For a more substantial dish, you could serve this with a sprout salad or noodles but it is also nice just to eat as a simple entrée.*

*You can also make a little herb salad for the side of the plate: mix parsley leaves, coriander leaves and baby rocket together and dress with a small amount of the dressing.*

# Seared Scallops with Wakame Seaweed, Witlof, Honey & Clove Dressing

100 g (3½ oz) Japanese eel, cut into 3 mm (¼ in) strips

3 witlof, julienned

3 red radishes, sliced thinly

100 g (3½ oz) baby watercress

100 g (3½ oz) large watercress

100 g (3½ oz) fresh wakame seaweed

18–24 scallops out of shell – no roe

## Tahini dressing

50 g (1¾ oz) tahini paste

25 ml (¾ fl oz) lemon juice

50 ml (1⅔ fl oz) water

sea salt and freshly ground black pepper

## Honey and clove dressing

100 ml (3½ fl oz) honey

100 ml (3½ fl oz) chardonnay vinegar

5 whole cloves

300 ml (½ pt) water

200 ml (7 fl oz) extra-virgin olive oil

## Sesame spice

20 g (1 tbsp) toasted ground nori

20 g (1 tbsp) toasted white sesame seeds

20 g (1 tbsp) toasted black sesame seeds

10 g (2 tsp) toasted bonito powder

**For the tahini dressing** Whisk tahini paste with lemon juice and water until dressing runs in a constant stream – you may not need to use all the water. Season, strain and set aside.

**For the honey and clove dressing** Place honey and chardonnay vinegar in a saucepan with cloves and simmer until reduced by a third. Whisk in water then olive oil. Strain and put aside.

**For the sesame spice** Mix ground nori, toasted white and black sesame seeds and bonito powder. Set aside.

Warm the eel strips, either in a low oven or microwave on low power. In a bowl mix the eel, witlof, radish, baby and large watercress and wakame seaweed, plus about a teaspoon of the nori and sesame spices, with honey and clove dressing. Place in the centre of 6 plates. Sear the scallops in a very hot pan (use a little olive oil if necessary) and place these around the plate. Drizzle tahini dressing over the top.

*Serves 6*

# Blinis with Caviar (or Salmon)

**Blinis**

200 ml (6½ fl oz) milk

7 g (¼ oz) dry yeast (1 standard sachet)

150 g (5 oz) plain flour

pinch of sea salt

2 eggs, separated

½ tbsp extra-virgin olive oil

**Topping**

2 eggs, hard-boiled

2 tbsp sour cream

2 tbsp beluga caviar or salmon roe,
or 6 slices of smoked salmon,
cut into thirds

handful of watercress for garnish

**For the blinis** Heat the milk to blood temperature. Sprinkle in the yeast and mix.

In a big mixing bowl, place the flour and salt. Add the egg yolks and the yeast mixture. Mix well with a wooden spoon. Place a damp tea towel over the top of the bowl and leave until batter doubles in size (at least half an hour).

Whisk or beat the egg whites until frothy and fold into the batter.

Heat the oil in a frying pan and ladle some mixture into the pan, to cover its base as thinly as you can (add more milk if mixture is too thick). Cook over a low heat until golden brown, then turn over to cook the other side for a couple of minutes. Remove from the pan and stamp out the blinis with a pastry cutter or the top of a glass (in circles of about 5 cm/2 in diameter). Repeat with the remaining mixture.

**For the topping** Finely mash the boiled egg (even push it through a sieve for a perfectly smooth texture). Mix with the sour cream.

*Makes about 18*

**To serve** *Spread the eggs over the blinis and top with a little caviar, salmon roe or smoked salmon (or top the smoked salmon with some caviar). Garnish with watercress and serve with champagne or sparkling wine.*

# Salmon Sashimi with Soy, Ginger & Shallot Dressing & Japanese Custard

200 g (6½ oz) sashimi-quality salmon, sliced

pinch of sea salt

¼ bunch chives, finely chopped

extra-virgin olive oil

### Custard

1 tbsp dashi soup stock granules

250 ml (8 fl oz) water

1 tsp mirin

½ tbsp soy sauce

½ tbsp sake

2 free-range eggs

### Dressing

50 g (1½ oz) shallots, finely chopped

50 g (1½ oz) ginger, finely chopped

1 tbsp soy sauce

Splash of extra-virgin olive oil

**For the custards** Preheat the oven to 130°C (260°F). Bring the dashi and water to the boil. Remove from heat and add the mirin, soy sauce and sake. Cool to room temperature. Whisk the eggs then whisk them into the dashi liquid. Strain and pour into 4 ¼-cup dariole moulds. (You can use ramekins.) Cover the moulds with aluminium foil, sit in a baking dish with hot water to come about 1 cm (½ in) up the moulds. Bake for 1¼ hours, or until just set. Cool and refrigerate until ready to serve.

**For the dressing** Mix together the shallots and ginger and leave for 1 hour for the flavours to infuse. Add the soy sauce and a little olive oil – just enough to make a paste consistency. Set aside.

*Serves 4*

*To serve Unmould the custards on to serving plates by running a hot knife around the edge to loosen the custard. Fan the salmon slices around the custard in a half-moon shape, season lightly with sea salt, and spread over some dressing. Sprinkle with chives and drizzle with extra-virgin olive oil.*

# Salt & Pepper Calamari

blended vegetable oil for deep frying

600 g (20 oz) calamari tubes

150 g (5 oz) flour

50 g (1¾ oz) sea salt, ground

50 g (1¾ oz) freshly ground pepper

Fill a large saucepan with oil and heat to 180°C (350°F).

Pat majority of moisture from the calamari. Cut down the side of each tube, flatten out and score outside with a dinner knife 2 mm (⅛ in) deep, in a criss-cross fashion. Slice into 2 cm x 4 cm (¾ in x 1½ in) pieces. Mix salt and pepper into flour and dust calamari pieces. Shake off excess flour and deep-fry calamari strips until golden and they start to twist. Drain on kitchen paper and serve with half a fat lemon.

*Serves 6*

**Note** *You can also serve this calamari with a dipping sauce made up of 1 part soy sauce to 2 parts olive oil.*

# Raw Tuna with Curry Dressing

250 g (8 oz) sashimi-quality tuna

sea salt to taste

2 sheets nori, julienned

1 bunch chives, chopped finely (about 60 g/2 oz)

**Curry dressing**

50 g (1¾ oz) coriander seeds

50 g (1¾ oz) cumin seeds

50 g (1¾ oz) fennel seeds

10 g (⅓ oz) chilli seeds (hot)

15 g (½ oz) ground turmeric

15 g (½ oz) ground cinnamon

2 whole cloves

10 cardamom pods

250 ml (8 fl oz) extra-virgin olive oil

100 ml (3½ fl oz) cabernet sauvignon vinegar

Begin preparations the day before you want to serve this dish.

Combine all the spices using a mortar and pestle with 50 ml (1⅔ fl oz) of the olive oil. Pound into a paste. In a heavy-based pot, dry fry paste over medium heat stirring constantly for 3 minutes. Add remainder of olive oil and bring to boil. Remove from heat and set aside to infuse overnight, before passing through a fine sieve.

**To make curry dressing** Pour vinegar into a bowl and whisk in the curry oil. Season to taste.

*Serves 6*

**To serve** *Slice the tuna thinly and divide between plates, slightly overlapping slices, and season. Drizzle the tuna with the dressing, sprinkle with julienned nori and chives.*

# Seared Scallops with Blue Cheese Polenta & Shiitake Mushrooms

50 g (2 oz) shiitake mushrooms

extra-virgin olive oil

12 medium–large scallops, roe removed

handful of watercress for garnish

truffle oil (optional)

**Polenta**

900 ml (1 pint 14 fl oz) water

pinch of sea salt

200 g (6½ oz) instant polenta

50 ml (1½ fl oz) cream

100 g (3½ oz) blue cheese
(e.g. Stilton)

salt and freshly ground black pepper

**For the polenta** In a saucepan combine a pinch of sea salt and water and bring to the boil. Pour in the polenta in a gradual steady stream, stirring constantly, and cook over low heat for 5 minutes. Stir in the cream, then crumble in the blue cheese and stir until melted through. Season to taste.

**For the shiitake mushrooms** Finely slice the mushrooms and blanch them in boiling salted water for about 30 seconds. Drain.

**For the seared scallops** Just before the polenta is ready, heat a heavy-based frying pan and add a little extra-virgin olive oil. When hot, add the scallops and cook until they are only just turning white, turning them once. The scallops will take less than a couple of minutes. Take care not to overcook them.

*Serves 4*

**To serve** Divide the polenta among 4 serving plates and flatten out a little with a knife. Top the polenta with a small pile of watercress, sprinkle the shiitake mushrooms on top and arrange the scallops around the watercress. Drizzle with a little truffle oil (optional).

*Serve with champagne or sparkling wine.*

# Yamba Prawn Tortellini

1 fresh corn cob

250 g (8 oz) prawn meat (peeled, tails and heads removed and deveined)

sea salt and freshly ground black pepper

1 bunch sage (about 60 g/2 oz)

18 gow gee wrappers

**Corn purée**

2 shallots

knob of butter

50 ml (1⅔ fl oz) white wine

1 yellow capsicum, chopped

2 x 425 g (14 oz) cans corn kernels

1 litre (1⅔ pt) milk

sea salt and freshly ground black pepper

**Sauce vierge**

100 ml (3½ fl oz) fish stock (see page 219)

100 g (3½ oz) butter

1 tbsp lemon juice

2 tsp capers

sea salt and freshly ground black pepper

2 tsp each of finely chopped flat-leaf parsley, chervil, lemon thyme

**For the corn purée** Peel shallots and finely chop them. Melt butter in a large saucepan and soften shallots gently in the butter. Add wine and allow to boil until reduced by half. Add chopped capsicum and canned corn, cover with milk and cook for 30 minutes. Strain vegetables, blend them together and season to taste.

Cook the fresh corn in salted boiling water. Once cooked slice the kernels from the cob. Chop prawn meat into 1 cm (½ in) cubes. Season prawn meat and mix with fresh corn kernels. Add 50 g (1¾ oz) of corn purée and mix to combine. Chop sage leaves and add to mixture. Place spoonfuls of the mix on gow gee wrappers, then fold in half so wrapper resembles a half moon. Stick the edges together by moistening with a little water. Now fold this semi-circle in half again, so the two edges on the flat side overlap. Stick down with a little water. Put tortellini aside.

**To make sauce vierge** Heat fish stock, add butter. Let butter melt, then add lemon juice and capers. Season to taste and add fresh herbs.

*Serves 6*

*To serve* Cook tortellini in boiling water for 5 minutes. Put a tablespoon of corn purée on each plate and put 3 tortellini on top. Spoon sauce over.

# Tempura Zucchini Flowers

18 zucchini flowers

rocket leaves

**Tempura batter**

200 g (7 oz) cornflour

100 g (3½ oz) plain flour

1 tbsp sea salt

300 ml (10 fl oz) lemon juice

iced water

**Stuffing**

350 g (12 oz) soft goat's cheese

200 ml (7 fl oz) cream

30 g (1 oz) pitted green olives, chopped

30 g (1 oz) preserved lemon rind (see page 223)

**For the batter** Mix flours and salt in a bowl and make a well. Slowly incorporate lemon juice in centre making a paste initially, then add iced water until batter is a thin, pouring consistency.

**To make stuffing** Soften goat's cheese by mixing it and slowly combining with the cream. Add chopped olives and lemon. Put mix into piping bag.

Take centres out of the flowers, pipe mix into the centres and pinch the top together. Refrigerate until the cheese is hard again. Coat with batter and deep fry in hot oil (180°C/350°F) until crispy.

*Serves 6*

*To serve* Divide between plates with a few rocket leaves.

*Notes* You can buy preserved lemon from most good delis or specialty stores.

*If zucchini flowers are out of season use the stuffing mix to fill a tart, with the addition of eggs.*

# Smoked Salmon & Jerusalem Artichoke Salad

200 g (6½ oz) Jerusalem artichokes, grated

½ bunch watercress

200 g (6½ oz) smoked salmon

**Dressing**

2 tbsp red wine or sherry vinegar

4 tbsp extra-virgin olive oil

squeeze of lemon juice

sea salt and freshly ground black pepper

**For the dressing** Combine all ingredients. Shake or whisk well.

**For the Jerusalem artichoke salad** Mix the artichokes and watercress, add the dressing and toss well.

*Serves 4*

*To serve* Lay the smoked salmon slices around the outside of a large serving plate, leaving a space in the middle. Pile the salad in the centre. Drizzle with a little extra-virgin olive oil.

# Warm Leek, Tomato, Red Capsicum & Sage Salad

4 vine-ripened tomatoes

2 red capsicums

8 sage leaves, finely sliced

1 tbsp red wine vinegar

1 tbsp extra-virgin olive oil

2 leeks, white part only

sea salt and freshly ground black pepper

**For the tomatoes and capsicums**
Preheat the oven to 200°C (400°F).

Cut the tomatoes into 6–8 wedges, place them in a shallow ovenproof dish and bake for 30–40 minutes.

Cut the capsicums into large pieces as flat as possible, removing the seeds and core. Place the pieces under a hot griller, skin-side up and close to the flame. Cook until the skin goes black and blistered (about 10 minutes). Put the pieces in a plastic bag and seal tightly. Leave for 5 minutes. Remove the capsicum and rub the skin off with your fingers. Slice finely.

When the tomatoes are well roasted, place in a bowl and add the capsicum strips and half the sage. Add the vinegar and extra-virgin olive oil and toss well. Set aside.

**For the leeks** Bring a saucepan of salted water to the boil. Cut the leeks in half lengthwise, in halves lengthwise again, then in halves horizontally, to form short batons. Drop into the boiling water and blanch for a couple of minutes. Drain.

*Serves 4*

*To serve* Place a pile of leeks on each plate, then carefully spoon a mound of tomato and capsicum mixture on top. Sprinkle with remaining sage and drizzle with a little extra-virgin olive oil. Season.

# Fig & Blue Cheese Salad

2 witlof, cut in half lengthwise

1 bunch (60 g/2 oz) chives

2 sticks celery

1 punnet (90 g/3 oz) watercress

1 cup (30 g/1 oz) white celery leaves

2 fresh figs

160 g (5 oz) blue cheese (e.g. Stilton)

**Dressing**

3 figs

½ tbsp butter

2 egg yolks

50 ml (1⅔ fl oz) red wine vinegar

50 ml (1⅔ fl oz) hazelnut oil

50 ml (1⅔ fl oz) extra-virgin olive oil

**To make the dressing** Preheat oven to 180°C (350°F). Slit the tops of 3 figs and stuff with butter. Wrap figs in foil and bake in oven for 10 minutes. Meanwhile whisk egg yolks and vinegar together until the mixture starts to thicken. Combine oils and slowly whisk oils into the yolks. Peel the figs, discard skin, roughly chop the flesh and add it to the dressing.

Chop the stalks off the witlof and chop chives into 2–3 cm (¾ in) lengths. Chop the celery in 4 mm (¼ in) thick slices on an angle. Mix all these together in a bowl with the watercress and celery leaves and gently toss through 2 tablespoons of the dressing.

*Serves 4*

*To serve* Break up figs, allowing half per person on each entrée plate. Using both hands delicately arrange salad on top of fig, then crumble a quarter of the cheese on each plate and drizzle remaining dressing over the whole salad.

**Note** You can vary the cheese you use in this salad. Although any blue vein will do, I think it would also be good with gorgonzola, and something like Italian fontina would produce a different effect.

# Watercress, Witlof, Pearl Barley & Blue Cheese Salad

200 g (6½ oz) pearl barley,
soaked in water for 24 hours

200 g (6½ oz) blue cheese (e.g. Stilton)

½ bunch watercress

50 ml (1½ fl oz) sherry vinegar

50 ml (1½ fl oz) walnut oil

50 ml (1½ fl oz) extra-virgin olive oil

1 large witlof

1 red capsicum

**For the pearl barley** Bring a saucepan of salted water to the boil. Drain the pearl barley, then rinse well under running water. Add to the boiling water and simmer for 1 hour, or until soft. Drain well and cool.

In a large bowl, mix together the pearl barley, crumbled blue cheese and watercress.

**For the dressing** Combine the vinegar, walnut oil and extra-virgin olive oil and shake or whisk well. Add to the pearl barley mixture and toss well.

**For the witlof** Separate the witlof spears, and cut each one in half vertically. Sprinkle on the base of a large serving plate.

**For the capsicum** Cut the red capsicum into small diamond shapes, about 1 cm (½ in) across. Set aside.

*Serves 4–6*

**To serve** *Pile the pearl barley mixture on top of the witlof, and sprinkle the plate with the red capsicum pieces.*

# Grilled Quail with Campari Jelly

6 jumbo quail, butterflied

**Jelly**

100 ml (3½ fl oz) Campari

2 tbsp sugar syrup (see page 226)

50 ml (1⅔ fl oz) orange juice

100 ml (3½ fl oz) tonic water

10 g (⅓ oz) allspice powder

3 gelatine leaves

1 cup (250 ml/8 fl oz) water

**Salad**

100 g (3½ oz) shiitake mushrooms, fresh

20 g (⅔ oz) ginger

250 g (8 oz) firm tofu, diced into 1 cm (½ in) pieces

1 bunch chervil, leaves picked off and washed (about 60 g/2 oz)

**To make the jelly** Mix Campari, syrup, orange juice, tonic water and allspice powder. Soak gelatine leaves in water until soft. Heat 50 ml (1⅔ fl oz) of the Campari mixture and add gelatine. Dissolve over a gentle heat. Add to rest of Campari mix, pour into a 250 ml glass (or similar) container and chill to set as a jelly.

**For the salad** Pan fry the shiitake mushrooms and allow to cool. Blanch the ginger in boiling water three times and then cut into julienne strips. To make salad, mix all ingredients.

Grill the quail for 4 minutes either side. Rest in a warm area for a few minutes.

*Serves 6*

**To serve** *Put a tablespoon of jelly on each plate, top this with a serving of salad, then put quail on top.*

**Note** *If fresh shiitake mushrooms are unavailable you can use the dried ones, just follow instructions for rehydration.*

# Chicken Liver Pâté with Preserved Orange & Rocket

*The preserved orange needs overnight refrigeration and is optional.*

**Pâté**

50 ml (1½ fl oz) port

50 ml (1½ fl oz) red wine

½ bunch thyme, leaves only

8 peppercorns

240 g (7½ oz) chicken livers

250 g (8 oz) clarified butter (see page 223)

3 free-range eggs

1 egg yolk

250 ml (8 fl oz) chicken stock (see page 221)

**Preserved oranges**

4 navel oranges

3 tbsp sea salt

200 g (6½ oz) sugar

2 tbsp treacle

60 ml (2 fl oz) sherry vinegar

250 ml (8 fl oz) water

4 star anise, broken up

12 peppercorns

2 cinnamon sticks, broken in half

12 cloves, crushed

pinch of nutmeg, grated or ground

1 tbsp sherry vinegar

2 tbsp extra-virgin olive oil

1 bunch rocket

6 or so slices brioche, toasted

**For the pâté** Combine the port, red wine, thyme and peppercorns in a small pan. Simmer until reduced by half. Strain and cool.

Preheat oven to 110°C (225°F). Bring livers, butter, eggs and yolk to room temperature. Place in a food processor, add the port reduction, and blend well. Push mixture through a sieve. Pour into ½-cup ramekins. Sit the ramekins in a baking tray in 1 cm (½ in) of hot water and bake for about 35 minutes, or until pâté feels firm when you gently tap its top. Cool.

Simmer chicken stock until reduced by half. Pour a little stock on top of the pâté to seal and place the ramekins in the fridge to chill.

**For the preserved oranges** Prick the oranges with a fork. Roll them in salt. Bring a large pan of water to the boil, drop the oranges in and boil for 15 minutes. Refrigerate overnight.

Quarter the oranges, leaving the skin on but removing the pips.

In a large saucepan, bring to the boil the sugar, treacle, sherry vinegar, water, star anise, peppercorns, cinnamon, cloves and nutmeg. Drop the orange quarters into the syrup and simmer gently for 20 minutes. Cool. Store oranges with their syrup in sterilised, sealed jars. Keeps for about 6 months.

**For the dressing** Whisk together the sherry vinegar and extra-virgin olive oil and toss the rocket in the dressing.

*Serves 6*

**To serve** *Place the ramekins of pâté on serving plates, add a slice of toasted brioche, a small handful of rocket and a little preserved orange (optional).*

# Roasted Duck Breast with Chestnut Salad & Dijon and Miso Dressing

2 muscovy duck breasts

25 g (¾ oz) brown sugar

25 g (¾ oz) Szechwan peppercorns

25 g (¾ oz) rock salt

### Salad

1 large turnip, peeled, quartered and thinly sliced

100 g (3½ oz) chestnuts, roasted and peeled

1 nashi pear, peeled, halved, cored and sliced into 0.5 cm (⅓ in) sticks

1 bunch baby watercress (about 60 g/2 oz)

sea salt and freshly ground black pepper

### Dressing

1 tbsp miso paste (red)

30 g (1 oz) Dijon mustard

2 tsp sherry vinegar

125 ml (4 fl oz) water

150 ml (5 fl oz) extra-virgin olive oil

pinch of sea salt

Ask butcher to trim duck breasts. Mix sugar, pepper and rock salt and cover duck breasts. Wrap in plastic film and refrigerate for 2 hours. Wash salt mix off and pat breasts dry.

**For the dressing** Put miso paste, mustard and sherry vinegar in a bowl. Slowly add half the water, until mixture is consistency of soup. Slowly whisk in olive oil until incorporated. Heat remaining water and add to dressing. Season.

**For the salad** Blanch turnip and place in bowl with chestnuts, pear and watercress. Season and dress with sufficient dressing to moisten, but reserving some dressing.

Preheat oven to 200°C (400°F). Place duck breasts skin side down in cold pan and heat over low heat until skin has crisped. Put into oven with other side uppermost for 3 minutes. Remove and let rest for 10 minutes.

*Serves 6*

**To serve** *Divide salad between plates. Slice breasts and arrange on top of salad, then spoon reserved dressing over everything.*

# Quail with Zucchini, Basil, Pine Nuts & Currants

4 quails (boned, but leaving on wings and drumsticks)

½ bunch (30 g/1 oz) thyme

zest of 1 lemon

extra-virgin olive oil

4 small zucchini

50 g (1¾ oz) butter

4 tbsp (80 g/2¾ oz) currants, soaked in port for at least 30 minutes

½ bunch (45 g/1½ oz) basil

2 tbsp (60 g/2 oz) pine nuts, lightly toasted

sea salt and freshly ground black pepper

extra-virgin olive oil, to drizzle

Rub quail with a mixture of thyme, lemon zest and enough olive oil to ensure the marinade coats the birds. Leave to rest for at least 1 hour in the fridge.

Grate zucchini. Melt butter in a pan and cook zucchini gently until softened. Add currants, the torn leaves of two-thirds of the basil (reserve rest for garnish) and pine nuts. Season.

Drain most of the oil from quail. Heat a pan until very hot and fry quail for 2–3 minutes on each side, then set birds aside to rest for 3 minutes.

*Serves 4*

**To serve** Place a mound of zucchini mixture on each plate, cut quail into quarters and sit the pieces on top. Garnish with extra basil and drizzle with olive oil.

**Notes** Quail is a tasty bird but it is important not to overcook it, or it will be tough.

Instead of frying, try grilling the quail on a barbecue, or use a hot plate on the barbecue. You can also bake them in a very hot oven.

Try to create height when serving, for a dramatic effect.

# Tempura of Quail, Wasabi & Sesame, Daikon, Watercress and Carrot

6 jumbo quail

100 g (3½ oz) brown sugar

100 g (3½ oz) rock salt

6 nori sheets

plain flour for dusting

2 litres cottonseed oil
(or similar light vegetable oil)

**Tempura batter**

200 g (7 oz) cornflour

150 g plain flour

2 egg yolks

pinch of sea salt

200 ml (7 fl oz) lime juice

100 ml (3½ fl oz) lemon juice

125 ml (5 fl oz) iced water

**Dressing**

5 tubes wasabi

1 tbsp sesame oil

60 ml (2 fl oz) soy sauce

600 ml (20 fl oz) extra-virgin olive oil

60 ml (2 fl oz) hot water

**Salad**

2 carrots

1 daikon radish

30 g (1 oz) butter

50 g (1¾ oz) honey

30 g (1 oz) sesame seeds

pinch of sea salt

1 punnet baby watercress
(about 90 g/3 oz)

Mix the brown sugar and rock salt together in a large bowl then cover the quail with this mixture for 15 minutes, to cure. Portion each quail into 4 pieces – 2 legs and 2 breasts. Brush the flat nori sheet with water and cut into quarters. Wrap each quail piece in nori.

**To make the batter** Put flours, egg yolks and salt in a bowl. Slowly add the citrus juices and water till pouring cream consistency. Strain through a coarse sieve.

Flour quail pieces, dip in batter and deep-fry in a wok or wok-based pan in preheated hot oil for approximately 2–3 minutes. Rest the quail in a warm place.

**To make the dressing** Squeeze the wasabi into a bowl. Whisk with sesame oil. Once combined, whisk in soy sauce. Once this has been combined whisk in olive oil, then hot water. Pour into 6 ramekins.

**For the salad** Peel carrot and daikon with a peeler into strips until the core is reached. Discard the core. In a pan heat butter, honey and sesame seeds until the sauce 'froths', add vegetable strips and quickly cook enough to soften them. Season and put into a bowl; mix through the baby watercress whilst vegetables are still hot.

*Serves 6*

***To serve*** *Reheat quail by plunging in hot oil for 1 minute and slice. Arrange quail, salad and dressing in a triangular pattern on plates.*

***Note*** *This makes a good amount of dressing which is fantastic on salads as well. It can be kept in an airtight container in the fridge for up to a month.*

# Persian Fetta & Rocket Tartlets

200 g (7 oz) savoury pastry
(see page 220)

50 g (2 oz) rocket

**Filling**

200 g (7 oz) Persian fetta

2 large eggs, beaten

2 dollops (1 tbsp) Greek yoghurt

sea salt and freshly ground
black pepper

**Rocket pesto**

90 g (3 oz) rocket

½ bunch (about 60 g/2oz)
English spinach

1 tbsp grated parmesan

1 tbsp toasted pine nuts

sea salt

juice of 1 lemon

50 ml (1⅔ fl oz) extra-virgin olive oil

Preheat oven to 180°C (350°F). Grease tartlet shells. Roll out pastry on a chilled and floured workbench (see Notes). Roll pastry back onto the pin and place on top of the shells. Mould pastry to shells and trim around the edges, then prick the base of pastry with a fork. Place moulds in freezer for about 10–15 minutes (this will stop pastry shrinking when you cook it). Bake in oven for 10 minutes. Cool on the bench and store in airtight container until ready for use.

Decrease the oven temperature to 175°C (345°F).

**To make the rocket pesto** Wash and pick any chunky stalks off the spinach and rocket. Blanch half the rocket and all of the spinach. Blend all ingredients except for oil, then add oil slowly, continuing to blend (if you add it too fast the pesto may separate). Check for seasoning: it may need a little more lemon juice and salt.

**To make the filling** Smash fetta with back of a spoon, add beaten eggs and combine, slowly mix through yoghurt and season to taste. Spoon into the baked pastry cases and cook for 4 minutes.

*Makes 15–20 small tartlets*

**To serve** *Put warm tartlets on plates with a drizzle of rocket pesto on top. Garnish with rocket leaves.*

**Notes** *Rocket pesto is also great as a dressing on salads or potatoes.*

*To chill a bench, fill a baking tray with ice and cold water and put tray on the bench for a few minutes: the bench will cool down and will be a suitable surface for working with pastry.*

# Zucchini, Red Onion & Basil Tarts

pastry for 4 savoury tartlet cases, about 10 cm (4 in) diameter (see page 220 or use frozen shortcrust pastry)

handful of dried beans or rice

4 small zucchini, finely sliced

4 small red onions, peeled and quartered

8 basil leaves, finely sliced

20 black olives, pitted

2 tbsp balsamic vinegar

2 tbsp extra-virgin olive oil, plus extra to drizzle

Preheat the oven to 200ºC (400ºF).

**For the tartlet cases** Lay the pastry into moulds and, using your fingers, gently press the pastry into shape. Trim the overhanging pastry with a sharp knife. Blind bake the tarts by cutting a piece of baking paper to about the size of the tartlet. Weigh down with a few dried beans or rice (this is to prevent the pastry from shrinking too much). Place in the oven for about 5 minutes.

Remove the beans or rice and baking paper, and return the tartlets to the oven for about another 5–7 minutes, or until cooked through and lightly golden. Remove from the oven and set aside.

**For the filling** Turn the oven down to 180ºC (350ºF). In a large bowl, mix together the zucchini, onions, half the basil, the olives, balsamic vinegar and extra-virgin olive oil. Transfer to a shallow ovenproof dish and bake for 15–20 minutes. Return the tart cases to the oven just before the vegetables are ready.

*Serves 4*

*To serve* Spoon the vegetable mixture evenly into the tart cases, sprinkle over the remaining basil and drizzle with extra-virgin olive oil.

# Mini Burgers with Beetroot Relish

**Burgers**

400 g (14 oz) good-quality minced beef

1 small onion, diced

1 egg

200 g (7 oz) breadcrumbs

sea salt

1 iceberg lettuce

**Beetroot relish**

40 g (2 tbsp) butter

20 ml (1 tbsp) honey

250 g (8 oz) raw grated beetroot

pinch of ground cinnamon

pinch of ground ginger

pinch of ground allspice

pinch of ground nutmeg

10 ml (2 tsp) sherry

50 ml (1⅔ fl oz) water

60 ml (2 fl oz) vinegar

**For the relish** Melt butter, dissolve honey in it and heat until caramelised and golden brown. Add grated beetroot and cook for 2 minutes, then add spices and sherry and cook for a few minutes longer. Add water and vinegar and continue to cook until beetroot is still a little crunchy.

Mix all burger ingredients together and roll into 12 balls. Flatten them out with your hand slightly.

Cook burgers in a frying pan, or under a hot griller, until cooked to taste.

*Serves 6*

**To serve** On each plate nestle two burgers in individual iceberg lettuce leaves, like little cups, with some beetroot relish on top.

**Notes** For hungrier people, or for lunch, make big burgers: just make the patties larger and serve on a damper roll with the beetroot relish.

*Leftover relish can be stored in a sterilised jar in the fridge.*

# BBQ Beef Fillet with Horseradish

2 bunches baby beetroot
(about 250 g/8 oz)

3 cloves garlic, peeled

50 ml (1⅔ fl oz) extra-virgin olive oil

30 ml (1 fl oz) chardonnay vinegar

½ bunch (about 45 g/1½ oz) tarragon

sea salt

2 tbsp horseradish relish

200 g (7 oz) sour cream

500 g (1 lb) beef fillet

freshly ground black pepper

90 g (3 oz) baby cress or watercress

Preheat oven to 180°C (350°F).

Try to select beetroots that are about the same size so they cook evenly. Cut the green tops off the beets and scrub with a scourer (you may want to use gloves) to remove all dirt. Thinly slice the garlic with a sharp knife and toss it with beets along with half of the olive oil and all the vinegar. Put beets in a baking tray and cover tightly with foil. Cook in oven for 30 minutes, then check to see if they are cooked: they will be ready when a knife goes through them easily. When they are cooked and still warm cut in half and toss them with the chopped tarragon and remaining oil. Season with salt.

Mix horseradish relish and sour cream together and refrigerate until ready to serve.

Season the beef fillet with salt and cracked black pepper and seal all sides on a hot barbecue or on a stovetop in a heavy-based cast-iron dish. Using a very sharp knife thinly slice the beef into slices 4–5 mm (¼ in) thick and flatten out, very thinly, with the back of your knife. If slices are large, cut in half or quarters.

*Serves 6*

**To serve** *Arrange a few slices of beef and beet halves on each plate, drizzle horseradish dressing over, scatter with cress and serve.*

# Rabbit Tarts with Polenta & Shiitake Mushrooms

4 rabbit fillets (or 2 chicken fillets)

1 tsp soy sauce

1 tsp sesame oil

pastry for 4 savoury tartlet cases about 10 cm (4 in) diameter (see page 220 or use frozen shortcrust pastry)

handful of dried beans or rice

250 ml (8 fl oz) chicken stock (see page 221)

2 cm (1 in) piece of ginger, peeled and halved

500 ml (1 pint) milk

100 g (3½ oz) instant polenta

50 ml (1½ fl oz) cream

50 g (1½ oz) Grana Parmigiana, grated

12 fresh shiitake mushrooms, quartered

chives, finely chopped, for garnish (optional)

Marinate the rabbit fillets in the soy and sesame oil for about 1 hour.

Preheat the oven to 200°C (400°F).

**For the tartlet cases** Lay the pastry into moulds and, using your fingers, gently press the pastry into shape. Trim the overhanging pastry with a sharp knife. Cut pieces of baking paper big enough to sit inside the cases, pour on a few beans or rice and blind bake the cases for about 5 minutes. Remove the paper and beans and cook for a further 5–7 minutes, or until cooked through and lightly browned. Remove from the oven.

**For the sauce** Pour the stock into a small saucepan with the ginger pieces. Cook over medium heat to reduce slightly and allow the ginger to infuse. Remove the ginger pieces and set aside.

**For the polenta** Bring the milk to the boil in a saucepan and pour in the polenta in a steady stream, stirring continuously. Turn the heat down to very low and stir for about 5 minutes, then stir in the cream and cheese. Turn off the heat, put a lid on to keep the polenta warm, and set aside.

Return the pastry cases to the oven on a low heat (120°C or 250°F) to warm through.

**Meanwhile, for the rabbit** On a char-grill or in a hot frying pan, cook the rabbit over high heat for 2–5 minutes. Remove from heat and rest.

In the same pan, sauté the mushrooms for a couple of minutes.

*Serves 4*

**To serve** Spoon some polenta into the warm tartlet cases to cover the base. Slice the rabbit (thickness of 3–5 mm/¼ in) and arrange on top of the polenta, overlapping the slices. Arrange a handful of mushroom on top of the rabbit and around the plates, and drizzle with the sauce. Garnish with chives (optional).

# Braised Suckling Pig

1.5 kg (3 lb) pork belly

200 g (7 oz) rock salt

200 g (7 oz) brown sugar

50 g (1¾ oz) star anise

1 cucumber

50 g (1¾ oz) table salt

1 green mango

1 cup Vietnamese mint leaves

1 cup coriander

## Stock

5 litres (8 pt) veal stock (see page 222)

1 litre (1⅔ pt) duck stock (see page 221)

zest of 1 orange

zest of 1 lemon

50 g (1¾ oz) ground cinnamon

Mix rock salt, sugar and star anise together. Coat pork belly with this mixture and leave for 2 hours. Wash coating off but retain star anise.

**To make the stock** Bring all stock ingredients to the boil in a large pot and add star anise, put pork in and cook with lid on for 4 hours or until pork is tender. Retain stock.

Remove pork from pot and discard sinew, cartilage and fat. Chill pork in fridge. When cool cut into triangles weighing about 100 g (3½ oz) each.

Preheat oven to 180°C (350°F). Heat a frying pan and seal each triangle on the side that had the fat on it until golden brown. Put triangles into an ovenproof dish with their unsealed sides facing up, and add sufficient stock to keep pork moist but do not cover the top of the meat. Bake in the oven for 30 minutes to glaze the top of the pork. The liquid should have reduced to a sauce.

Peel and de-seed the cucumber, and julienne it into 10 cm (4 in) lengths. Cover the cucumber with table salt and let sit for 15 minutes. Rinse salt off and drain cucumber. Peel the mango and grate its flesh, and mix with cucumber and torn mint leaves.

*Serves 4–6*

*To serve* Place cucumber mix in the centre of individual serving bowls or plates. Put pork on top and spoon the sauce over the pork. Garnish with coriander sprigs.

# Eggs & Cheese

# Scrambled Eggs on Brioche with Crab Meat

6 free-range eggs

100 ml (3½ fl oz) milk

100 ml (3½ fl oz) cream

pinch of sea salt

cracked black pepper

1 tbsp butter

4 slices brioche

120 g (4 oz) fresh crab meat

½ bunch chives, finely chopped

**For the scrambled eggs** Lightly whisk the eggs, mix in the milk and cream, and season to taste with salt and pepper. Melt the butter in a saucepan and pour in the egg mixture. Heat slowly, stirring continuously.

**Meanwhile** Toast the brioche and place a slice on each plate.

*Serves 4*

*To serve* When the eggs are three-quarters cooked, spoon them on to the side of the brioche – they should still be creamy. Place a small mound of crab meat next to the eggs, and sprinkle the plates with chives.

# Fine-herb Omelette

**Per person**

1 tsp extra-virgin olive oil

3 free-range eggs

1½ tbsp finely chopped herbs
(e.g. chervil, chives, parsley, tarragon)

25 ml milk (1 fl oz)

25 ml cream (1 fl oz)

sea salt and freshly ground black pepper

watercress for garnish

**For each omelette** Heat the oil in a small frying pan. In a small bowl, whisk the eggs, stir in the herbs, milk and cream and season well. Pour the egg mixture into the pan and roll it around to achieve as thin an omelette as possible.

Using a spatula, start folding in the sides of the omelette and gradually roll it right up – this should take only 2–3 minutes.

*To serve* Slide each omelette on to a serving plate and garnish with watercress.

# Asparagus with Poached Egg, Parmesan & Truffle Oil

32 asparagus spears,
woody ends trimmed

4 free-range eggs

4 tbsp (80 g/2 ¾ oz) shaved parmesan

drizzle of truffle oil
(or good extra-virgin olive oil)

sea salt and freshly ground
black pepper

Using a potato peeler, scrape away the bottom third of the asparagus spears. Blanch asparagus in boiling salted water for 2 minutes. Drain. Place 8 spears on each warmed serving plate.

Poach the eggs until just cooked, ensuring the yolks are still runny. Slide an egg on top of the asparagus. Sprinkle with parmesan and drizzle with truffle oil. Season to taste.

*Serves 4*

**Note** *Another way to remove the woody stem from the asparagus is hold a spear in the middle and snap its end off: the spear should break just where it begins to get woody.*

# Poached Eggs with Cucumber & Dill Sour Cream

**Cucumber and dill sour cream**

½ telegraph cucumber

200 ml (6½ fl oz) sour cream

1 bunch dill, finely chopped

2 tbsp water

**Poached eggs**

1 tbsp vinegar

pinch of sea salt

8 free-range eggs

**For the cucumber and dill sour cream** Using a potato peeler, cut the cucumber into fine ribbons. Set aside.

In a small bowl, mix the sour cream and dill together. Add about 2 tbsp water and mix well to make a dressing consistency.

**For the poached eggs** Bring a small pot of water to the boil and then simmer gently. Add vinegar and a pinch of salt and swirl the water around to create a whirlpool effect. This helps to keep the eggs from breaking up when poaching.

Crack the eggs into the water, 2 at a time, and cook for about 3 minutes (for runny yolks, longer if desired).

Lift out of the water with a slotted spoon.

*Serves 4*

*To serve Put 2 eggs on each plate. Mix a small handful of cucumber with some dressing and place on top of the poached eggs. Drizzle more dressing over the eggs and around the plate.*

51

# Ocean Trout with Poached Egg & Spinach

4 fillets of ocean trout

pinch of sea salt

1 bunch English spinach

3 medium potatoes, peeled

**Poached eggs**

splash of vinegar

4 free-range eggs

100 ml (3½ fl oz) hollandaise sauce (see page 222)

sea salt and freshly ground black pepper

**For the ocean trout** Heat the oven to 200°C (400°F). Place the trout in a shallow tray and bake until just heated through (about 10 minutes).

**Meanwhile** Bring three saucepans of salted water to the boil.

**For the spinach** In one saucepan, blanch the spinach, drain and keep warm.

**For the potatoes** In another saucepan, boil the potatoes until cooked but still firm. Drain and slice the potatoes into matchstick shapes, as finely as you can. Keep warm.

**For the poached eggs** In the third saucepan, add a splash of vinegar to the water. Swirl the water to create a whirlpool and add the eggs, 2 at a time. Poach for about 3 minutes, until cooked but with runny yolks.

*Serves 4*

**To serve** *Place a pile of potato in the centre of the plates, put some spinach on top, then the trout, then a poached egg and dollop with hollandaise sauce. Season well.*

# Crêpes Filled with Sweet Potato Soufflé

**Crêpes**

250 g (8 oz) plain flour

sea salt

3 eggs

500 ml (2 cups) milk

butter

**Soufflé**

500 g (1 lb) sweet potato, peeled, boiled and puréed

100 ml (3½ fl oz) cream

4 eggs, separated

100 g (3½ oz) grated parmesan

sea salt and freshly ground black pepper

90 g (3 oz) rocket

50 g (2 oz) parmesan, shaved

25 ml (1 fl oz) white wine vinegar

100 ml (4 fl oz) extra-virgin olive oil

**To make the crêpes** Sift the flour and salt into a bowl. Make a well in the middle and crack in the eggs. Add the milk and whisk until smooth. Leave to rest for 5–10 minutes.

In a non-stick frypan, heat a little butter and brush over the base and sides of the pan. Ladle in enough crêpe mixture to just cover the base of the pan, tipping pan as you add mixture around to make the crêpe as thin as possible. Cook until lightly browned, then turn and cook the other side. Slide out of the pan. Repeat until all the mixture is used (should make about 6 crêpes). Crêpes can be made in advance and kept, covered, in the fridge until needed.

Preheat oven to 180°C (350°F).

**To make the soufflé** In a large bowl combine the sweet potato and cream (the mixture should be firm, not wet and gooey). Beat egg yolks and add, mix well. Beat the whites until stiff peaks form and fold through the mixture, along with the parmesan. Season to taste.

On heatproof serving plates (or a greased, flat tray) lay a crêpe so that half of it is hanging over the side. Spoon about 4 heaped tablespoons of sweet potato mixture onto the crêpe, fold crêpe over to make a half-moon shape and cook in the oven for about 10 minutes, or until the soufflé puffs up.

*Serves 6 as an entrée*

**To serve** *Mix rocket and parmesan. Whisk vinegar and oil to make dressing and toss salad. Divide salad between plates and add crêpe.*

**Note** *You can vary the soufflé filling for the crêpes – replace the sweet potato with mashed potato and grated gruyère cheese, or use two parts potato/gruyère to one part puréed beetroot, broccoli, peas or asparagus (all passed through a sieve).*

# Spinach & Ricotta Parcels

2 bunches (about 300 g/10½ oz) spinach, blanched and drained well

300 g (10½ oz) ricotta

½ bunch (about 30 g/1 oz) chives, chopped

½ bunch (about 45 g/1½ oz) basil, chopped

2 tbsp toasted pine nuts

2 tbsp currants

½ tsp freshly grated nutmeg

sea salt and freshly ground black pepper

½ packet filo pastry

20 g (1 tbsp) butter, melted

black sesame seeds

Preheat oven to 180°C (350°F).

Squeeze spinach to ensure it is dry, then mix with ricotta and chopped herbs. Smash pine nuts with back of a heavy knife, chop currants and mix both into spinach and ricotta with nutmeg. Season to taste.

Take 3 sheets of filo pastry and cut into squares. Put some filling on one half of the square, brush some melted butter around the edge – the outer 0.5 cm (¼ in) – and turn unfilled half of pastry over filling to make a triangle. Continue making triangles until filling has been used up. Brush tops of triangles with melted butter and sprinkle with sesame seeds.

Cook in oven until golden brown (approximately 5 minutes).

*Makes 10–15*
*(depending on size of parcels)*

*Notes* These can be made in advance, so you can just throw them in the oven at the last moment.

*Make whatever shape you want, but I think triangles are always a winner.*

*Whole nutmegs should be available at the supermarket. It is worth the effort to grate one's own freshly as you need it, as fresh nutmeg has a distinctive flavour, very different to the packaged ground spice.*

# Tuna, Tomato & Herb Frittata

8 free-range eggs

250 ml (8 fl oz) cream

95 g (3 oz) canned tuna, drained

1 tomato, roughly chopped

1 tbsp finely chopped fresh mixed herbs

sea salt and freshly ground
black pepper

1 tsp butter

1 tsp extra-virgin olive oil

Preheat the oven to 150°C (300°F).

Whisk the eggs and cream together.
Add the tuna, chopped tomato and
mixed herbs. Season and mix well.

Heat the butter and extra-virgin olive
oil in a frying pan. Pour in the egg
mixture and cook over a low heat until
the bottom has set. Finish off the
cooking by placing the pan in the oven
for 15–20 minutes, or until just set.
(If your frying pan will not fit in your
oven, or has a non-heatproof handle,
finish off the frittata under the griller.)

*Serves 2 generously*

**To serve** *Remove the pan from the
oven, cut the frittata in half and
serve on plates immediately.*

# Gruyère on Sourdough Toast

4 thick slices sourdough bread

160 g (5 oz) gruyère cheese, grated

5 tbsp chopped parsley

extra-virgin olive oil

Toast one side of the bread under
the griller. In a bowl, mix together
the cheese and parsley. Pile on to the
untoasted sides of the bread and return
to the griller until lightly coloured.

*Serves 2*

**To serve** *Drizzle a little extra-virgin
olive oil over the grilled cheese and
serve with a glass of good red wine.*

# Goat's Cheese Tart with Preserved Lemon & Green Olives

1 quantity (about 300 g/10 oz) savoury pastry (see page 218 or use frozen shortcrust pastry)

6 eggs

350 ml (11 fl oz) cream

500 g (1 lb) soft goat's cheese

100 g (3½ oz) preserved lemon, skin removed and flesh chopped (see page 223)

100 g (3½ oz) pitted green olives

sea salt and freshly ground black pepper

1 bunch rocket

extra-virgin olive oil

Preheat oven to 180°C (350°F). Grease a quiche dish measuring about 27 cm (11 in) in diameter. Line it with pastry, trimming around the top with a sharp knife and then prick the pastry base well with a fork. Blind bake the tart case by cutting a piece of baking paper to about the size of the tart. Lay it on the pastry and weigh it down with a small handful of dried beans or rice. Place case in the oven for 5 minutes. Remove the beans or rice and paper and discard, and return the pastry to the oven for a further 5–7 minutes, or until cooked through and lightly golden.

**To make the filling** In a large bowl whisk together the eggs and cream. Crumble in the goat's cheese, add preserved lemon and green olives and mix well. Season to taste. Pour into the pastry case and bake for 10–15 minutes, or until just set.

*Serves 6*

**To serve** *Cut into wedges, top each with rocket and drizzle with olive oil.*

# Tomato, Basil & Cheddar Tarts

savoury pastry for 4 tartlet cases about 10 cm (4 in) diameter (see page 220 or use frozen shortcrust pastry)

handful of dried beans or rice

100 g (3½ oz) butter

6 vine-ripened or roma tomatoes, quartered

1 bunch basil, finely sliced

sea salt and freshly ground black pepper

200 g (6½ oz) aged cheddar cheese, grated

1 bunch rocket

extra-virgin olive oil

Preheat the oven to 200°C (400°F).

**For the tartlet cases** Lay the pastry into moulds and, using your fingers, gently press the pastry into shape. Trim the overhanging pastry with a sharp knife. Blind bake the tarts by cutting a piece of baking paper to about the size of the tartlet. Weigh down with a few dried beans or rice (to prevent the pastry from shrinking too much). Bake for about 5 minutes in the oven.

Remove the beans or rice and baking paper, and return the tartlets to the oven for about another 5–7 minutes, or until cooked through and lightly golden. Remove from oven and let cool.

**For the filling** Heat the butter in a frying pan or heavy-based saucepan over medium heat. Add the tomatoes and toss until they start to break down (about 5 minutes). Add half the basil, season to taste, transfer to a heatproof dish and place in the oven, uncovered, for 7 minutes.

Place the tomato/basil mix in a mixing bowl and fold through the grated cheese.

Spoon the mixture into the tartlet cases and return to the oven for a further 7 minutes, or until the cheese forms a gratin topping.

*Makes 4*

**To serve** *Place each tart on a serving plate, garnish with a small pile of rocket and the remaining basil and drizzle with a little extra-virgin olive oil.*

# Roasted Vegetable Frittata

450 g (15 oz) desirée potatoes, diced

450 g (15 oz) pumpkin, diced

extra-virgin olive oil

sea salt and freshly ground
black pepper

6 eggs

200 ml (7 fl oz) cream

1 cup (about 60 g/2 oz)
parsley leaves, chopped

1 tsp butter

Preheat oven to 200°C (400°F).

Cut potatoes and pumpkin into similar sized cubes so they cook evenly (potatoes will take longer than the pumpkin). Toss in olive oil, salt and pepper and roast in hot oven until three-quarter cooked (approximately 30 minutes, depending on size of vegetables). Leave to cool. Reduce oven to 150°C (300°F).

Beat eggs and mix with cream and chopped parsley. Melt butter in an ovenproof non-stick pan, add egg mix then arrange cooked vegetables in the pan (make sure you don't over fill because mix will rise) and cook over low heat until the bottom has set. Cook in oven until just set in the centre and golden brown – about 15–20 minutes. If you don't have a suitable ovenproof pan you can finish frittata under the grill.

*Serves 4*

**Notes** *If there is any leftover egg mixture make another, smaller one.*

*Using the same egg and cream quantities you can make any flavour of frittata you like. For instance: mixed cheeses and herb; bacon, onion, potato and parmesan; roasted red onion, capsicum and fetta.*

*Frittata is great served hot or cold, so is ideal for a picnic.*

# Zucchini Slice

3 large zucchini
(about 400 g/14 oz in all)

1 onion

2 rashers bacon (about 100 g/3½ oz)

20 g (1 tbsp) butter

40 g (1⅓ oz) pecorino

40 g (1⅓ oz) parmesan

4 free-range eggs

125 g (1 cup) self-raising flour

sea salt and freshly ground
black pepper

Preheat oven to 180°C (350°F).

Grate zucchini, peel and dice onion and chop the bacon. Melt butter and gently soften onion in it until beginning to become translucent, then add the bacon and cook for a couple of minutes more. Remove from heat and chill.

While the bacon and onion mix chills grate the cheeses. Crack the eggs in a bowl and beat lightly.

Mix together the grated zucchini, bacon mix, cheeses and flour. Combine this mix with the eggs. Season if needed.

Pour into a greased, shallow tin and bake for 30 minutes.

*Serves 6 as a light meal,
10 as a good snack*

**Notes** *This is great hot or cold.*

*The recipe is exactly the same as my mum's – except she used tasty cheese! I quite often have a few different cheeses in my fridge and like the combo of pecorino and parmesan.*

# Welsh Rarebit

250 g (8 oz) cheddar cheese, grated

185 ml (6 fl oz) pale ale

1 tsp English or Dijon mustard

splash of Worcestershire sauce

1 free-range egg yolk

4 thick slices bread

In a saucepan heat the cheese, beer, mustard and Worcestershire, stirring well. Whisk in the yolk and keep stirring until the cheese has completely melted and the ingredients are well combined. Don't worry that it is runny – it will firm up under the griller.

Toast four chunky bread slices and butter them.

*Serves 2*

**To serve** *Place 2 slices of toast on each plate, or shallow bowl/plate, pour the cheese mixture over the top of the toast, then place the plates under the griller until the top is browned. Serve immediately.*

# Pasta & Rice

# Penne with Black Olives, Basil & Mascarpone

pinch of salt

400 g (14 oz) penne pasta

400 g (14 oz) mascarpone

100 ml (3½ fl oz) cream

150 g (5 oz) black olives,
pitted and chopped

100 g (3½ oz) parmesan cheese, grated

1 bunch basil, roughly chopped

sea salt and freshly ground
black pepper

Bring a large pot of salted water to the boil. Add the pasta and cook until al dente.

**Meanwhile** In another saucepan, bring the mascarpone and cream to the boil then turn the heat down to a gentle simmer. Add the olives, parmesan cheese and all but 1 tbsp of basil. Mix well. Season.

Drain the pasta, and tip it back into the hot pot. Pour in the creamy sauce and toss well.

*Serves 4*

**To serve** *Scoop the pasta into bowls and sprinkle the remaining basil on top.*

# Spaghetti with Stir-fried Beef, Tomato & Snowpea Sprouts

300 g (10 oz) beef sirloin,
sliced into strips

8 tomatoes

2 tbsp extra-virgin olive oil

1 large onion, finely chopped

1 clove garlic, crushed

50 ml (1½ fl oz) dry white wine

500 g (1 lb) spaghetti, or
pasta of your choice

½ bunch flat-leaf parsley,
finely chopped

1 punnet snowpea sprouts

sea salt and freshly ground
black pepper

In a frying pan, sauté the beef. Remove from the pan and set aside.

**For the tomatoes** Bring a large pot of salted water to the boil. Score the skin of the tomatoes and blanch for about 30 seconds; remove with a slotted spoon and refresh in cold water. Peel off the skin, cut into quarters and use a spoon to scrape out the seeds. Roughly dice the flesh. (Don't tip out the water – you can use it for the pasta.)

Heat the extra-virgin olive oil in the frying pan, add the onion and garlic and cook for a few minutes. Pour in the wine and simmer until reduced by half. Add the tomato and cook for 4–5 minutes.

**For the pasta** Bring the tomato water to the boil again and add the pasta. Cook until al dente.

Just as the pasta is ready, add the beef to the tomato mixture and heat through. Toss through the parsley and snowpea sprouts.

*Serves 4*

**To serve** *Drain the pasta and tip it back into the hot pot. Pour over the sauce, season and toss through.*

# Linguine with Smoked Salmon & Dill Cream Sauce

**Dill cream sauce**

1 tbsp extra-virgin olive oil

1 onion, finely chopped

150 ml (5 fl oz) dry white wine

250 ml (8 fl oz) fish (or chicken) stock (see page 219)

300 ml (10 fl oz) cream

sea salt and freshly ground black pepper

350 g (12 oz) pasta (e.g. linguine, fettuccine)

1 bunch English spinach

150 g (5 oz) smoked salmon (or 3 slices per person)

½ bunch dill, finely chopped

**For the sauce** Preheat the oven to 220°C (425°F).

Heat the extra-virgin olive oil in a large saucepan. Add the onion and cook until soft. Add the wine and simmer over medium heat for a minute or so until it reduces slightly. Add the stock and simmer for a couple more minutes, then the cream and simmer again for a few minutes until it thickens slightly. Season well.

**Meanwhile, for the pasta** Bring a large saucepan of salted water to the boil and add the pasta. Cook until al dente. Drain. Just before the pasta is ready, blanch the spinach in boiling water. Drain and keep warm.

*Serves 4*

*To serve* Pile the pasta evenly into serving bowls. Lay 3 slices of smoked salmon over each bowl of pasta and put them in the oven for a couple of minutes to just heat the salmon. Add half the dill to the sauce, stir, and pour over the pasta and salmon. Place a small handful of spinach on top and sprinkle with the remaining dill.

# Penne with Mushrooms & Oregano

400 g (14 oz) penne pasta

2 tbsp butter

1 tsp extra-virgin olive oil

1 red onion, peeled and sliced

400 g (14 oz) field or button mushrooms, sliced

125 ml (½ cup) white wine

125 ml (½ cup) cream

2 tsp chopped oregano or parsley

sea salt and freshly ground black pepper

chopped chives for garnish (optional)

Bring a large pot of salted water to the boil. Add the pasta and cook until al dente.

While the pasta is cooking, in another large saucepan heat the butter and olive oil, add the onion and cook until soft. Add the mushrooms and cook for 2–3 minutes. Pour in the wine and simmer until the liquid has reduced by half. Stir in the cream and bring to the boil. Add the herbs, switch off the heat and season to taste.

*Serves 4*

**To serve** *Drain the pasta, tip it into the mushroom pan and toss it all together. Serve garnished with chopped chives (optional).*

# Risotto Base

1 tbsp butter

1 tbsp extra-virgin olive oil

1 onion, peeled and finely chopped

400 g (14 oz) arborio rice

250 ml (1 cup) white wine

1 litre (4 cups) hot chicken stock
(see page 221) or vegetable stock

sea salt and freshly ground
black pepper

Heat the butter and olive oil together in a large heavy-bottomed pan over medium heat. Add the onion and cook until soft. Add the rice and stir for a minute or two until well coated with the oil and butter. Add the wine and stir until it is absorbed.

Start adding the hot stock, a ladleful or two at a time. With each addition of stock, stir steadily and constantly until the liquid has been absorbed. Keep adding the stock gradually and stirring constantly until the rice is plump and creamy, cooked but still slightly al dente (this takes about 20–25 minutes). Season to taste.

*Serves 4*

# Fennel & Pea Risotto

Risotto ingredients (see above)

1 fennel bulb, finely sliced

375 g (1½ cups/13 oz) frozen peas

fennel tops, roughly chopped (optional)

125 g (½ cup/4 oz) grated parmesan

Five minutes before the risotto base is ready (that is after about 15–20 minutes stirring), add the fennel, peas and fennel tops. Continue stirring and adding stock until the rice is al dente. Just before serving, stir through the parmesan.

*Serves 4*

# Beetroot Risotto

Risotto ingredients (see page 69)

450 g (15 oz) beetroot, puréed

125 g (½ cup/4 oz) grated parmesan

4 tsp horseradish cream

chopped chives for garnish

**To prepare beetroot** Bake in foil (at 180°C/350°F) for about 20 minutes or until the beetroot is soft. Allow to cool, unwrap and remove skins. Chop and purée adding some water if necessary.

**To make horseradish cream** Use one part cream to three parts horseradish relish.

Cook risotto (see page 69). Five minutes before the risotto base is ready (that is, after about 15–20 minutes stirring), stir through the puréed beetroot. Continue stirring and adding any remaining stock until the rice is al dente. Just before serving, stir through the parmesan.

*Serves 4*

*To serve Spoon into bowls and top with a teaspoon of horseradish cream. Garnish with chopped chives.*

# Pumpkin & Pancetta Risotto

Risotto ingredients (see page 69)

2 tbsp extra-virgin olive oil

45 g (1½ oz) butter

4 sprigs rosemary

1 clove garlic, peeled

600 g (20 oz) pumpkin flesh, diced

10 slices pancetta

125 g (½ cup/4 oz) grated parmesan

In a pan heat olive oil and butter together. Add half the rosemary, the garlic and pumpkin. The pumpkin will release a little liquid so there is no need to add any water. Cover pan and cook on low heat for 20 minutes, until the pumpkin softens and dissolves. Take rosemary and garlic out and rest.

Chop pancetta and fry in a pan until crispy. Drain on kitchen paper and set aside. Cook risotto (see page 69).

*Serves 4*

*To serve When risotto is ready, stir pumpkin through the base and serve topped with the pancetta, parmesan and the rest of the rosemary, chopped.*

# Leek & Blue Cheese Risotto

1 tbsp extra-virgin olive oil

1 tbsp butter

1 onion, finely chopped

1 leek, white part only, finely sliced

400 g (14 oz) arborio rice

250 ml (8 fl oz) dry white wine

1 litre (2 pints) fish stock
(see page 221) or vegetable stock, hot

150 g (5 oz) soft blue cheese, crumbled

sea salt and freshly ground
black pepper

Heat the extra-virgin olive oil and butter in a large, heavy-bottomed saucepan. Sauté the onion and leek until soft.

Add the rice and stir for a few minutes to coat with the oil and butter. Pour the wine into the pan and stir the rice until it has been absorbed. Start adding the hot stock, a ladle or two at a time. With each addition of stock, stir constantly until the liquid has been absorbed. Keep gradually adding the stock and stirring constantly until the rice is creamy but still al dente (about 30–35 minutes).

*Serves 4*

**To serve** *Just as the risotto is ready for serving, stir in the blue cheese. Season and stir well. Put the lid on the pan and allow to rest for a few minutes before serving.*

# Mushroom Risotto

**Mushroom stock**

2 kg (4 lb) field mushrooms

sprig of thyme

1 clove garlic

1 stick celery, chopped

1 onion, finely chopped

**Risotto**

30 g (1 oz) butter

1 onion, finely chopped

250 g (8 oz) arborio rice

125 ml (4 fl oz) white wine

1 litre (2 pints) mushroom stock (or chicken stock – see page 221), hot

3 tbsp grated Grana Reggiano

100 g (3½ oz) mixed mushrooms (e.g. field, shiitake, enoki), sliced

2 tbsp chopped fresh mixed herbs

1 tbsp butter, plus extra

extra-virgin olive oil

**For the stock** Place the field mushrooms on 2 baking trays and bake in the oven at 150°C (300°F) for 1 hour.

Then place the mushrooms in a large saucepan, cover with water and add the thyme, garlic, celery and onion. Simmer for about 1 hour, topping up with water every now and then if necessary. Strain. Pour into a saucepan and keep hot.

**For the risotto** Melt the butter in a large, heavy-based saucepan. Add the onion and cook until it softens. Add the rice and stir for a few minutes until well coated. Add the wine and stir until it is absorbed.

Add a ladleful of hot stock, and stir constantly until it is absorbed. Continue adding stock, a ladleful at a time, and stir constantly until the rice is plump and creamy, cooked but without being too soft (about 30–35 minutes).

To finish, stir in the cheese, mushrooms, and all but a teaspoon of herbs. Add the spoon of butter, switch off the heat, put the lid on the pan and leave to rest for a few minutes.

*Serves 4*

*To serve Drizzle extra-virgin olive oil and sprinkle herbs on top.*

*Note The mushroom stock is time-consuming but you will be rewarded with intense flavour.*

# My Paella ~ or Seafood Risotto

250 ml (1 cup) white wine

1 tsp saffron threads

40 g (2 tbsp) butter

1 onion, peeled and finely diced

500 g (1 lb) calaspara rice
(Spanish paella rice, available
from specialised delis)

1.5 litres (2½ pt) hot fish stock
(see page 221)

1 x 450 g (15 oz) can roma
tomatoes, strained and diced

300 g (10 oz) mussels,
scrubbed and debearded

200 g (7 oz) green raw prawns, peeled

200 g (7 oz) scallops, roe removed

sea salt

lemon juice

handful of chopped fresh herbs
(e.g. dill, parsley, basil)

For this recipe you can use a
large sauté pan with a lid or
a cast-iron Dutch oven.

Heat wine in a pan and add
saffron; set aside to infuse.

Melt butter and gently cook onion
until soft but not coloured. Add the
rice and stir for 5 minutes. Add wine
and saffron, stir until wine is absorbed,
then add 1 ladleful of hot stock, stir
until absorbed, and repeat until the rice
is almost cooked (15–20 minutes).
At this stage add a little more stock,
the diced, strained tomatoes and the
seafood. Put the lid on and steam the
seafood for about 5 minutes, shaking
the pan to stop everything sticking.
Take the lid off check that the rice and
seafood is cooked, season with salt and
a squeeze of lemon juice and stir through
chopped herbs. Serve immediately.

*Serves 4–6*

*Notes* Paella has been a favourite of mine
*since going to Spain. It can be a very*
*complicated dish – this is my easy version.*

*You can use risotto rice (arborio) or long*
*grain if it is not possible to get calaspara.*

*Use seafood that is available fresh:*
*just make sure whatever seafood*
*ingredients you choose have*
*about the same cooking time.*

# Pan-fried Barramundi with Preserved Lemon & Basil Risotto & Sweet Pea Sauce

6 x 150 g (5 oz) barramundi fillets

extra-virgin olive oil

**Risotto**

100 g (3½ oz) butter

1 onion, peeled and finely chopped

500 g (1 lb) arborio rice

100 ml (3½ fl oz) white wine

2 litres (3¼ pt) hot fish stock
(see page 221)

1 tbsp lemon thyme, chopped

1 cup basil, chopped, plus
6 leaves for garnish

½ cup flat-leaf parsley, chopped

1 tbsp chervil, chopped

150 g (5 oz) good quality parmesan,
finely grated

sea salt

30 g (1 oz) preserved lemon
(see page 223)

**Sweet pea sauce**

20 g (1 tbsp) butter

1 small onion, peeled and sliced

50 ml (1⅔ fl oz) white wine

600 ml (20 fl oz) fish stock
(see page 221)

500 g (1 lb) frozen peas

sea salt and freshly ground
black pepper

**To make the sauce** Melt butter in a medium pan and gently cook onion until softened, add white wine and boil until liquid has reduced by half. Add hot fish stock, bring to boil and add peas. Cook for 3 minutes, season, strain and reserve liquid. Purée in a blender, adding enough reserved liquid to achieve a soup consistency. Set aside.

**To make the risotto** Melt 30 g (1 oz) butter in a large, heavy-based pan and cook onion gently until softened but not browned. Add rice and stir constantly until grains are hot. When hot, add white wine and cook until liquid is almost evaporated. Turn down heat and gradually add hot fish stock, a ladleful at a time, stirring the rice constantly. As rice takes up the liquid, add more stock until the rice is cooked – approximately 30 minutes. Add chopped herbs. Fold parmesan cheese, a little salt, herbs, preserved lemon and remaining butter into risotto. Check seasoning and adjust if necessary.

Preheat oven to 180ºC (350ºF). Pan-fry barramundi in a little olive oil until lightly browned on both sides, then put in pre-heated oven for 5–7 minutes.

*Serves 6*

*To serve* Put a serving of risotto on 6 plates with a barramundi fillet atop. Pour pea sauce around risotto and garnish with julienned strips of reserved basil leaves.

# Seared Scallops with Spanish Onion & Caper Risotto

70 g (2½ oz) butter

1 onion, finely chopped

200 g (6½ oz) arborio rice

50 ml (1½ fl oz) white wine

750 ml (1½ pints) fish or
chicken stock (see page 219), hot

½ Spanish onion, finely sliced

2 tsp finely chopped mixed herbs

1 tbsp Grana Parmigiana, grated

2 tsp small (liliput) capers

24 scallops, roe removed

sea salt and freshly ground
black pepper

extra-virgin olive oil

**For the risotto** In a large, heavy-based saucepan, melt two-thirds of the butter, add the chopped onion and cook until soft. Add the rice and stir for 5 minutes. Add the wine and stir until absorbed. Start to ladle in the hot stock, a ladle at a time, constantly stirring until it is absorbed by the rice.

Keep adding the stock slowly, continually stirring, until the rice is almost cooked (about 30–35 minutes).

Add the Spanish onion, herbs, cheese and capers and stir through. The rice should be creamy, the grains al dente. Put a lid on the pan and leave the risotto to rest for a few minutes while you cook the scallops.

**For the scallops** Season the scallops and sear them in a hot frying pan until browned on the outside but only just cooked through – they take only 1–2 minutes and are ready when they turn from opaque to white.

*Serves 4*

**To serve** *Place a neat mound of risotto on each serving plate and arrange 6 scallops per person around the risotto. Drizzle with extra-virgin olive oil.*

# Fish & Seafood

# Prawn, Witlof, Raisin & Parsley Salad

4 heads witlof

50 g (1½ oz) butter

1½ tbsp sugar

200 ml (6½ fl oz) veal or chicken stock (see pages 222, 221)

1 tbsp butter, extra

16 green (raw) king prawns, peeled but with tail intact

2 bunches parsley, leaves roughly chopped

150 g (5 oz) raisins

25 ml (1 fl oz) balsamic vinegar

sea salt and freshly ground black pepper

**For the witlof** Separate the witlof spears and cut each in half vertically. In a pan over high heat, add the butter and sugar and stir until the sugar has dissolved to make a light caramel. Add the witlof to the pan and brown a little. Add the stock and cook until the witlof is tender (2–3 minutes).

**Meanwhile, for the prawns** Remove any black intestinal tract. In a heavy frying pan melt extra butter and sauté the prawns in the hot pan until they just turn from transparent to white.

Toss the parsley, raisins and prawns together with the balsamic and season well.

*Serves 4*

*To serve Place a little pile of witlof on each plate, and drizzle with pan juices. Pile the prawn mixture high on top of the witlof.*

# Chilli Prawns

3 large chillies

½ bunch (about 45 g/1½ oz) coriander

2 limes

50 ml (1⅔ fl oz) honey

200 ml (7 fl oz) extra-virgin olive oil

16–20 green prawns,
peeled but tails left on

De-seed and dice the chillies. Roughly chop coriander, and mix with the zest and juice of the limes and the honey. Add the olive oil. Put prawns in the marinade and leave for 30 minutes, then barbecue or put on an ovenproof tray and grill. Prawns are cooked when they turn from green to pink.

*Serves 4*

**Notes** *This is an easy one I give to the boys with beers. We eat them straight off the tray most of the time, but if you want to be a little more civilised, put a fingerbowl on the table, sprinkle some chopped coriander leaves over the cooked prawns and offer some steamed rice on the side.*

*You can vary the marinade with garlic or sweet chilli sauce if you can't be bothered with chillies.*

*If you like prawns really hot just add more chillies.*

# Crisp Calamari with Lemon & Caper Mayonnaise

400 g (14 oz) fresh calamari,
cleaned and finely sliced into rings

plain flour for coating the calamari

oil for shallow (or deep) frying

sea salt and freshly ground
black pepper

½ bunch watercress

1 lemon, quartered

**Mayonnaise**

200 ml (6½ fl oz) fresh
mayonnaise (see page 225)

50 ml (1½ fl oz) freshly
squeezed lemon juice

1 tbsp capers
(preferably the tiny liliput capers)

**For the mayonnaise** Add the lemon juice and capers to the mayonnaise. Mix well. Refrigerate until ready to serve.

**For the calamari** Heat the oil, either in a deep-fryer (if you have one) or in a shallow frying pan, until smoking. Toss the calamari rings in seasoned flour and fry until golden brown (about 3 minutes). Remove and drain on paper towel.

*Serves 4*

**To serve** *Season the calamari and serve with a dollop of mayonnaise, a handful of watercress and a lemon wedge.*

# Skewers of Scallops & Prawns with Tamarind Dressing

1 packet bamboo skewers

400 g (14 oz) peeled green (raw) prawns

400 g (14 oz) scallops, roe removed

**Dressing**

75 g (2⅔ oz) tamarind

350 ml (11 fl oz) hot water

60 ml (3 tbsp) honey

sea salt

Dissolve tamarind in hot water. Using disposable gloves squeeze the pulp to help the process. Pass through a sieve and discard pulp. Whisk honey into tamarind water and season with salt.

Soak bamboo skewers for at least an hour so they don't burn whilst cooking. Thread prawns and scallops onto skewers one after the other until full. Cook on barbecue until prawns are pink.

Serve dressed with tamarind dressing on a bed of steamed couscous, or with a herb and sprout salad.

*Serves 4*

*Note You can also skewer monkfish and prawns and/or baby octopus.*

# Calamari with Tarragon Pesto & Eggplant

2 bunches tarragon

400 g (14 oz) fresh calamari,
cleaned and sliced into rings

2 cloves garlic, crushed

2 small eggplant,
finely sliced into rounds

sea salt and freshly ground
black pepper

## Pesto

2 tbsp pine nuts

2 tbsp grated parmesan

about 100 ml (3½ fl oz)
extra-virgin olive oil

**For the calamari** Remove the leaves
from the tarragon bunches (for the
pesto) and keep the stalks. Marinate
the calamari in the stalks and the
crushed garlic for 30–45 minutes.

**For the pesto** In a pan, toss the pine
nuts over medium heat until lightly
browned. In a food processor, blend
the tarragon leaves, toasted pine
nuts, parmesan and enough oil to
make a pesto consistency. Set aside.

Char-grill or sear the eggplant in a hot
frying pan in a little extra-virgin olive
oil. Keep warm. Sauté the calamari
in the pan until just cooked through
(about 3 minutes). Season well.

*Serves 4*

**To serve** *Lay the eggplant slices around
the plates, sprinkle the calamari on top
and drizzle around the pesto dressing.*

# Steamed Whiting Fillets on Sweetcorn Pancakes

sea salt and freshly ground
black pepper

8 whiting fillets

240 g (8 oz) green beans, trimmed

**Pancakes**

150 g (5 oz) plain flour

75 ml (2½ fl oz) milk

25 ml (1 fl oz) extra-virgin olive
oil, plus extra to drizzle

2 free-range eggs

1 egg yolk

125 g (4 oz) corn kernels

2 tbsp chopped parsley,
plus extra for garnish

**For the pancakes** Place flour in a
large mixing bowl and make a well in
the centre. Add the milk, oil, eggs and
yolk to the well and whisk together
all the ingredients until smooth. Fold
in the corn and parsley. Season.

**For the fish** Season the fish and
steam for about 6 minutes, or until
just cooked through. If you don't have
a steamer, place in a shallow dish
covered with buttered foil and bake at
200°C (400°F) until cooked through.

**Meanwhile, for the pancakes**
While the fish is cooking, add a little
extra-virgin olive oil to a frying pan
and when hot, ladle in the pancake
batter to a diameter of about 10
cm (4 in) across for each of the 4
pancakes. When one side is lightly
browned, flip over and cook through.

Plunge the beans into a saucepan
of boiling water for a few minutes,
then drain and season.

*Serves 4*

**To serve** *Place a pancake in the
centre of each plate, place some beans
on top of that, then lay 2 whiting
fillets over the beans in a cross shape.
Sprinkle with parsley and drizzle
with a little extra-virgin olive oil.*

# Tuna with Curried Lentils

4 tuna steaks

handful of baby spinach
leaves for garnish

extra-virgin olive oil

### Curried lentils

30 g (1 oz) butter

2 onions, finely chopped

300 g (10 oz) green Puy lentils

750 ml (1½ pints) fish or
chicken stock (see page 221)

extra 100 g (3½ oz) butter

2 tbsp curry powder (buy a good blend
or make up your own e.g. ground chilli,
cumin, coriander, turmeric, fenugreek)

**For the lentils** Melt the butter in a
large saucepan. Add the onions and
cook until soft. Add the lentils, stir
well, then pour in the fish stock. Bring
to the boil, turn down to a simmer,
and cook until al dente (about 20
minutes). You should have 125 ml
(4 fl oz) of stock left in the pan.

In another saucepan, melt the
extra butter and add the curry
mix, stirring well. Add lentils
and the stock and stir well.

**For the tuna** Char-grill or sear
the tuna in a hot frying pan until
well coloured on the outside but
rare inside (or cook as desired).

*Serves 4*

**To serve** *Spoon the lentils into large
shallow bowls or plates, place the
tuna on top, spoon over any extra
juice, place a few baby spinach
leaves on top of the fish and drizzle
with extra-virgin olive oil.*

# John Dory with Asparagus & Cider Dressing

pinch of sea salt

2 bunches asparagus,
woody ends trimmed

½ bunch watercress

sea salt and freshly ground
black pepper

4 John Dory fillets

1 tbsp extra-virgin olive oil

1 tsp butter

**Dressing**

50 ml (1½ fl oz) cider vinegar

50 ml (1½ fl oz) apple juice

100 ml (3½ fl oz) extra-virgin olive oil

1 tsp cream

Preheat the oven to 200°C (400°F).

**For the dressing** Whisk together
the vinegar, apple juice, extra-virgin
olive oil and cream. Set aside.

**For the salad** Bring a saucepan
of salted water to the boil for the
asparagus. Drop the spears in the
boiling water for about 3 minutes.
Drain. In a large bowl, mix the
asparagus with the watercress, add two-
thirds of the dressing and toss well.

**For the John Dory** Season the fish
fillets. Add the oil and butter to a
frying pan over medium heat. Sear
the fillets on both sides for a couple of
minutes, then transfer to an ovenproof
dish and place in the oven for 4–5
minutes, or until just cooked through.

*Serves 4*

**To serve** *Place some asparagus and
watercress salad next to the fish on
each serving plate, and drizzle both
with the remaining cider dressing,
drizzling a little around the plate, too.*

# Steamed John Dory with Field Mushrooms & Bacon

50 g (1½ oz) butter

2 small brown onions, finely sliced

250 g (8 oz) bacon, sliced
into small batons

2 large field mushrooms, thickly sliced

6 large kipfler potatoes,
peeled and diced

750 ml (1½ pints) fish stock or
chicken stock (see page 219)

1 bunch flat-leaf parsley, finely chopped

4 John Dory fillets

extra-virgin olive oil

sea salt and freshly ground
black pepper

Melt the butter in a heavy-based pan. Cook the onions until soft. Add the bacon and cook for a few more minutes. Add the field mushrooms and potato. Pour in enough stock to just cover the mixture and simmer until the potato is soft (about 6–7 minutes). Stir in all but 1 tbsp of parsley.

**For the John Dory** Just before the mushroom mixture is ready, place the fish fillets in a bamboo steamer, drizzle with extra-virgin olive oil and season. Steam for about 4 minutes, or until just cooked through. (Or cook the fish in a shallow dish in the oven if you don't have a steamer, drizzled with oil, seasoned and covered with buttered foil.)

*Serves 4*

**To serve** *Spoon the mushroom mixture on to serving plates, place a fillet of John Dory on top and garnish with remaining parsley.*

# Blue-eye Cod Stuffed with Shallots & Thyme, Caramelised Witlof

12 shallots, finely chopped

60 g (2 oz) unsalted butter

splash of dry white wine

½ bunch thyme, leaves only

4 blue-eye cod fillets, skin on if possible

sea salt and freshly ground black pepper

extra 1 tbsp butter

2 punnets snowpea sprouts

## Witlof

70 g (2½ oz) unsalted butter, plus extra 1 tbsp

100 g (3½ oz) sugar

4 heads witlof, leaves halved lengthwise

100 ml (3½ fl oz) fish stock (see page 219)

Melt the butter in a frying pan and add the shallots with the wine and thyme. Cook until the shallots are soft. Set aside.

**For the blue-eye cod** Preheat the oven to 220°C (425°F).

If your cod has skin, using a sharp knife make an incision under the skin to form a pocket. If your fillets have no skin, use the knife to cut a pocket into the fillet horizontally. Using your fingers, fill the pocket with the shallot mixture. Season the fish with salt and pepper.

Melt the knob of butter in a pan over medium to high heat and brown both sides of the cod. Transfer to a heatproof dish and place in the oven to finish cooking through (about 5 minutes).

**Meanwhile, for the witlof** Melt the butter with the sugar in a saucepan over low heat, stirring, until the sugar has dissolved and a light caramel forms. Add the witlof and fish stock and cook until the witlof has softened.

In another pan, melt the extra butter and sauté the snowpea sprouts for a couple of minutes.

*Serves 4*

*To serve* Place a small pile of witlof in the centre of the plate, with a spoonful or 2 of the caramel juices. Sit a handful of snowpea sprouts on the witlof and place the fish on top.

# Baked Cod Fillets with Tomato, Ginger & Coriander

6 x 150 g (5 oz) blue-eye cod fillets, skin on (or any firm white-fleshed fish)

**Salsa**

6 roma tomatoes

sea salt

1 large red chilli

1 tbsp ginger, peeled

½ bunch (about 45 g/1½ oz) coriander

1 tbsp white wine vinegar

1 tbsp extra-virgin olive oil

Preheat oven to 200°C (400°F).

**For salsa** Score the bottom of the tomatoes and blanch in salted, boiling water for 30 seconds or until the skin starts to come away. Take out of the water and plunge into iced water. When cool peel the tomatoes, cut in half and squeeze the seeds out with your hand. Chop the tomatoes into about 1 cm (⅓ in) dice and season with salt.

Cut the chilli in half lengthwise, scrape the seeds out then finely dice flesh and add to the tomato. Grate the ginger using the fine side of the grater and add to the tomatoes. Pick the coriander leaves from the stems and chop them, then stir into tomato mixture, together with vinegar and oil. Check seasoning.

**To cook the fish** Heat a small amount of oil in a frying pan. When the oil is hot place fish fillets in skin side down and fry until skin is brown – approximately 2 minutes. Remove to a greased tray and cook in oven for another 5 minutes. When the fish is cooked the flesh will be white and flaky.

*Serves 6*

**To serve** Serve on dinner plates with a generous spoonful of salsa.

**Notes** This is a very simple and light way to serve fish. You could also serve with a side dish of crispy potatoes.

The salsa can be served with other fish dishes. Try a teaspoon on oysters or as a side salad.

# Coral Trout with Soba Noodles & Enoki Mushrooms

2 tbsp miso paste

310 ml (10 fl oz) water

3 tbsp brown sugar

75 ml (2½ fl oz) dry sake

8 coral trout fillets (or red emperor)

300 g (10 oz) soba noodles

1 tbsp extra-virgin olive oil

100 g (3½ oz) enoki mushrooms

400 g (14 oz) snowpea sprouts

800 g (1 lb 10 oz) bean sprouts

1 bunch coriander, chopped

Mix together the miso paste and water to make a miso stock, add the sugar and sake and stir well. Marinate the trout in this liquid for about 12 hours.

Preheat the oven to 200°C (400°F).

**For the soba noodles** Bring a large pot of water to the boil. Add the noodles, return to the boil, add 250 ml (8 fl oz) of cold water, return to the boil, add another 250 ml (8 fl oz) of cold water, return to the boil once more, then taste to make sure noodles are cooked through. Drain and rinse well under running water. Set aside.

**For the coral trout** Remove the fish from the marinade. Strain the marinade through a fine sieve into a small saucepan. Bring to the boil then simmer, ready to pour over the fish.

Heat the extra-virgin olive oil in a frying pan and seal the fish on one side, then flip to seal the other. Transfer to an ovenproof dish and place in the oven to cook (about 5 minutes). Just before the fish is due to be ready, in the frying pan sauté the mushrooms lightly.

**Meanwhile, for the sprouts** While the fish is cooking, bring a saucepan of boiling water to the boil. Add the snowpea sprouts and bean sprouts for a couple of minutes. Drain immediately and toss with the soba noodles and coriander.

*Serves 4*

**To serve** *Divide the noodle mixture among 4 bowls, lay the fish over the noodles, put some mushrooms on top of the fish and pour over the hot miso marinade.*

# Pan-fried Snapper with Mussels, Cucumber & Tomatoes

700 g (1½ lb) mussels (optional)

4 x 200 g (7 oz) snapper fillets, skin on

sea salt

50 ml (1⅔ fl oz) white wine

extra-virgin olive oil

## Cucumber and tomato salad

1 cucumber

4 vine-ripened tomatoes

sea salt

25 ml (1 fl oz) white wine vinegar

¼ bunch (about 20 g/⅔ oz) dill

¼ bunch (about 20 g/⅔ oz) basil

40 ml (1⅓ fl oz) extra-virgin olive oil

**To make the salad** Cut cucumber lengthwise and de-seed. Cut tomatoes in half and de-seed as well. Dice tomato and cucumber into 2 cm (¾ in) cubes and season with sea salt. Add the vinegar, roughly chopped dill, torn basil leaves and olive oil.

De-beard the mussels and give a light scrub with a clean scourer if they aren't already clean. Salt skin of snapper fillet and place skin side down in a hot pan and cook for 3 minutes on each side. Take out of pan and rest.

While the fish is resting throw the mussels in the same pan, pour in wine and cover pan. Boil vigorously. The steam will open the mussels: they are cooked when they open.

*Serves 4*

**To serve** *Put fish and mussels on dinner plates with cucumber salad to the side and drizzle with olive oil.*

**Notes** *This is a very fresh and tasty meal, but also quick to prepare. The fresher the mussels are the better it will be.*

*Discard any mussels that don't open.*

*You can also cook the fish and mussels on the barbecue. If you coat the mussels with wine before putting them on the barbecue they will cook really quickly.*

# Tuna with Roasted Tomato & Asparagus Purée

4 vine-ripened tomatoes

extra-virgin olive oil

4 tuna steaks

12 basil leaves for garnish

**Asparagus purée**

2 bunches of asparagus,
woody ends trimmed

200 ml (6½ fl oz) fish stock
(see page 219)

**For the tomatoes** Preheat the
oven to 200°C (400°F).

Cut each tomato into 6 wedges and
place in a shallow ovenproof dish.
Drizzle over a little extra-virgin olive
oil and roast for about 20–25 minutes.

**Meanwhile, for the asparagus purée**
Bring the fish stock to the boil and
add the asparagus. Simmer until very
soft. Drain almost all the stock off,
but keep a few tablespoons to put in a
blender with the asparagus. Purée the
mixture in the blender until smooth.

Just before the tomatoes are ready,
sear the tuna in a very hot frying
pan, or on a char-grill, until coloured
on the outside but rare inside.

*Serves 4*

**To serve** *Place 6 tomato wedges on
each plate, place a tuna steak on
top, dollop some purée on top of the
tuna, garnish with 3 basil leaves and
drizzle with extra-virgin olive oil.*

# Tuna with Onion Crème, Thyme, Asian Greens & Mussels

20 mussels (optional)

4 x 200 g (6½ oz) tuna steaks

300 g (10 oz) mixed Asian greens
(e.g. bok choy, choy sum)

extra-virgin olive oil

**Onion crème**

2 tbsp butter

6 onions, finely chopped

1½ tbsp white wine

50 ml (1½ fl oz) fish or chicken stock
(see page 219)

100 ml (3½ fl oz) cream

½ bunch thyme, leaves only

**For the onion crème** Melt the
butter and sweat the onions over a
gentle heat until soft. Add the white
wine and allow to reduce a little,
then add the fish stock. Simmer
for a few minutes to reduce a little
more, then add the cream. Stir in
the thyme leaves. Keep warm.

**For the mussels** If you are serving
the tuna with mussels, scrub them
well and remove their beards. Discard
any that are open. In a large saucepan
bring a little water to the boil. Add
the mussels, cover the saucepan tightly
and boil for a minute or so. Remove
the opened mussels and set aside.
Throw out any that do not open.

**For the tuna** Sear the tuna on
both sides in a hot frying pan until
well coloured but rare inside.

Blanch the Asian greens in a
saucepan of boiling water for
about 2 minutes. Drain.

*Serves 4*

*To serve* Place a large spoonful of
onion crème on a plate. Place the tuna
on top of the crème, then top with the
greens. Drizzle with extra-virgin olive
oil and serve the mussels to the side.

# Barbecued Tuna with Corn Salsa

4 x 200 g (7 oz) tuna steaks

**Salsa**

3 corn cobs

1 onion, diced

1 red capsicum, diced

1 tbsp extra-virgin olive oil

1 large red chilli, de-seeded
and finely chopped

¼ bunch (1 tbsp) tarragon, chopped

¼ bunch (1 tbsp) dill, chopped

¼ bunch (2 tbsp) parsley, chopped

zest of 1 lime

30 ml (1 fl oz) extra-virgin olive oil

sea salt

Slice corn off the cobs. Soften the onion and capsicum in oil, then add chilli and corn and cook gently for about 8 minutes, stirring occasionally. Take off the heat and add herbs, lime and extra-virgin olive oil. Season to taste.

Sear the tuna on the barbecue or in a very hot griddle pan for a few minutes on each side until it is cooked through. Serve with a couple of tablespoons of salsa.

*Serves 4*

**Notes** *Salsa can be served hot or cold but it is best at room temperature.*

*This is a very fresh, summery dish that doesn't take very long to prepare, because the salsa can be made in advance.*

*The salsa is good accompanying leftovers.*

*Salsa can be used with salmon, tuna and swordfish as well as meats and chicken.*

# Salmon with Celery-vanilla Stock

4 salmon fillets

2 bunches asparagus,
woody ends trimmed

8 tiny white onions, peeled

100 g (3½ oz) peas

1 bunch chervil, finely chopped

**Celery-vanilla stock**

300 ml (10 fl oz) fish stock
(see page 221)

150 ml (5 fl oz) freshly
squeezed celery juice

3 vanilla beans, split vertically

sea salt and freshly ground
black pepper

**For the stock** Heat the fish stock,
add the celery juice and vanilla beans
and simmer for a few minutes. Season.

**For the salmon** Steam the salmon
for 5–6 minutes or heat the oven
to 200°C (400°F) and bake
in a shallow dish covered with
buttered foil. Keep warm.

**For the vegetables** Bring a
saucepan of salted water to the
boil and blanch the vegetables for
a few minutes, until just tender.

*Serves 4*

**To serve** *Divide the vegetables between
4 bowls or bowl-plates, place the salmon
on top and pour over the celery-vanilla
stock. Sprinkle with chervil.*

# Salmon with Spiced Couscous, Green Olive Tapenade & Mascarpone

4 salmon fillets

500 ml (1 pint) fish stock (see page 221)

1 tbsp extra-virgin olive oil

250 g (8 oz) couscous

2 tbsp harissa

sea salt and freshly ground black pepper

40 Roman beans

200 g (6½ oz) green olive tapenade

100 g (3½ oz) mascarpone

25 ml (1 fl oz) extra-virgin olive oil

Remove any bones from salmon. Set aside.

**For the spiced couscous** Heat the fish stock. Heat the extra-virgin olive oil in a saucepan until smoking. Add the couscous and mix well, toasting until golden brown (3–4 minutes). Stir in the harissa, then pour in the fish stock and keep stirring until the stock has been absorbed. Season well, cover and set aside.

**For the salmon** Place the salmon in a steamer and cook for 5–6 minutes, or until just cooked. If you don't have a steamer, heat the oven to 200ºC (400ºF) and bake in a shallow dish covered with buttered foil.

**For the Roman beans** Bring a saucepan of salted water to the boil and cook the beans for a couple of minutes. Drain.

**For the mascarpone** Lightly mix the olive tapenade with the mascarpone.

*Serves 4*

*To serve* Fork the couscous and place a round mound on each plate, place the salmon on top, with the beans and a dollop of mascarpone next to it. Drizzle with extra-virgin olive oil.

# Barramundi with Cauliflower Purée, Zucchini, Basil, Pine Nuts & Currants

50 ml (1½ fl oz) extra-virgin olive oil, plus extra to drizzle

4 barramundi fillets

sea salt and freshly ground black pepper

2 tbsp pine nuts

4 small zucchini, cut into matchsticks

4 tbsp currants, marinated in a little port

12 basil leaves, sliced finely

## Cauliflower purée

2 tbsp butter

1 cauliflower, florets only (remove stalks), finely sliced

1 litre (2 pints) milk

sea salt and freshly ground black pepper

Preheat the oven to 180°C (350°F).

**For the cauliflower purée** Melt the butter in a large, shallow pan. Add the cauliflower and cook over a gentle heat, stirring occasionally, for about 10 minutes. Just cover the cauliflower with milk (you may not need to use the whole litre) and simmer gently until tender. Drain, purée and season.

**Meanwhile, for the barramundi** Heat the oil in a frying pan. Season the barramundi and cook on one side until golden brown, flip over to colour the other side, then transfer to an ovenproof dish and finish off in the oven for 4–5 minutes. While the fish is cooking through, add the pine nuts to the pan and stir until lightly toasted. Add the zucchini and currants and stir for a couple of minutes, then throw in the basil. Season.

*Serves 4*

*To serve* Spoon some purée on to the plates in a round shape, place the barramundi on top, then the zucchini mixture on top of the fish. Drizzle with a little extra-virgin olive oil.

# Mahi Mahi with Figs & Blue Cheese Sauce

4 x 100 g (3½ oz) mahi mahi fillets

4 figs

1 bunch asparagus (about 250 g/8 oz)

1 bunch pencil leeks, washed

baby basil leaves (about ½ cup)

**Blue cheese sauce**

100 ml (3½ fl oz) cabernet
sauvignon vinegar

100 g (3½ oz) fourme d'ambert
(or any mild blue cheese)

150 ml (5 fl oz) fish stock
(see page 221)

**Crust**

150 g (5 oz) almond slivers, toasted

100 g (3½ oz) ginger, finely grated

1 cup basil leaves

4 cloves garlic

1 cup milk

15 g (½ oz) butter

sea salt

**To make the crust** After almonds are toasted, allow to cool and place in food processor. Pulse for about 5 seconds and add basil and ginger. Pulse for about 10 seconds and put mix into a bowl. Put garlic in the milk, bring to the boil and simmer until garlic is soft – about 10 minutes. Strain garlic and squeeze pulp into the almond and basil mix. Melt butter and add to mix, making a paste. Season with sea salt.

**To make the sauce** Put the cabernet sauvignon vinegar into a pan with half the blue cheese and the fish stock. Heat and allow to reduce, whilst whisking constantly so cheese melts, until volume is half the original quantity. Set aside.

Preheat oven to 180°C (350°F). Slice figs into 5 slices each, on a bias. Put figs on a baking tray lined with baking paper and cook in oven until semi-collapsed – about 5 minutes.

Wash the asparagus and leeks. Snap the woody end off the asparagus spears and discard. Slice both asparagus and leeks on bias, then blanch.

Season fish and press the almond crust over one side. Place on a baking tray lined with baking paper and cook in the preheated oven for 7 minutes.

*Serves 4*

**To serve** *Divide the figs between plates with leek and asparagus on top. Place the mahi mahi on top and pour the sauce around. Divide the remaining cheese into a dozen knobs, put 3 on each plate, and decorate with baby basil leaves.*

**Note** *If mahi mahi isn't available you can try swordfish.*

# Mahi Mahi with Parsley Crust, Crispy Prosciutto & Corn

6 x 150 g (5 oz) mahi mahi cutlets

200 g (7 oz) prosciutto

## Crust

200 g (7 oz) day-old bread, toasted

¼ bunch (about 20 g/⅔ oz) sage, chopped

½ bunch (about 60 g/2 oz) flat-leaf parsley, chopped

30 g (1 oz) grated parmesan

2 tsp Dijon mustard

1 egg

1 egg yolk

sea salt

## Corn sauce

1 onion, peeled and diced

150 g (5 oz) white-fleshed fish scraps

100 ml (3½ fl oz) white wine

1 x 425 g (13 oz) can corn kernels

200 ml (2 fl oz) cream

3 cobs corn

sea salt and freshly ground black pepper

lemon juice (optional)

**For the crust** Process bread until a doughy consistency, add herbs, parmesan cheese and mustard. Remove from processor and slowly add eggs until it is a moist dough. Check seasoning. Pat this dough crust to a thickness of 0.5 cm (¼ in) around each portion of fish.

**For the corn sauce** Sweat onion (cook gently) in a pan until translucent. Add fish scraps and cook until sealed. Add wine and heat until volume is reduced by half, then add the canned corn kernels and cream. Simmer for 15 minutes. Blend to a purée and sieve, set aside.

Barbecue or grill fresh cobs of corn until golden brown, slice kernels off the cobs.

Preheat oven to 200°C (400°F). Place fish cutlets on an oiled oven tray and bake for 15 minutes or until the flesh is white. Roughly slice prosciutto into strips and fry until crispy, drain on kitchen paper.

When nearly ready to serve, reheat sauce then add fresh kernels. Season sauce and add a little lemon juice if necessary.

*Serves 6*

**To serve** Place 3–4 tablespoons of sauce in the centre of each plate, put fish on top and sprinkle with fried prosciutto.

**Notes** The trick to serving fish is not to overcook it. Don't be afraid to check with a knife to see if it is cooked enough before you serve. However, it is better if the fish is a little underdone rather than overdone, because you can always cook it some more if necessary.

# Whole Fish with Asian Greens & Crab Meat

4 plate-sized barramundi
(or any plate-sized fish)

extra-virgin olive oil

3 shallots, peeled and diced

2 tsp ginger, grated

2 kaffir lime leaves, chopped

200 g (7 oz) shiitake mushrooms, sliced

½ Chinese cabbage, shredded

15 ml (½ fl oz) fish sauce

50 ml (1⅔ fl oz) fish stock
(see page 221)

200 g (7 oz) crab meat

lime wedges to serve

### Coating

1 sheet nori (Japanese seaweed)

2 tsp sesame seeds

2 tsp dried chilli, chopped

Preheat oven to 200°C (400°F).

Tear nori into small pieces, and mix with sesame seeds and chilli. Pat the coating liberally around each fish. Seal fish in a hot pan, transfer them to an ovenproof dish and cook in the oven for approximately 8 minutes.

While the fish is cooking heat oil in a large frying pan, add shallot, ginger, lime leaves and mushrooms. Add cabbage and sauté for 3 minutes, add the fish sauce, stock and crab meat and simmer until the cabbage collapses.

*Serves 4*

*To serve Serve fish on dinner plates with a small amount of Asian greens on top, letting the sauce drip over the fish, and a wedge of lime on the side.*

# Poultry

## Chicken, Duck & Quail

# Barbecued Quails with Peach Salsa

8 quail

extra-virgin olive oil

**Peach salsa**

5 peaches

1 red onion

½ bunch (about 45 g/1½ oz) Vietnamese mint

½ bunch (about 45 g/1½ oz) basil

30 ml (1 fl oz) white wine vinegar

20 ml (1 tbsp) extra-virgin olive oil

pinch of sea salt

For salsa, blanch peaches in boiling water, then refresh in iced water and peel. Cut peaches through the centre, pull apart and discard the stones, then chop peaches in 1.5 cm (½ in) dice. Finely dice the onion and chop the herbs; add these to the peaches. Add the vinegar, olive oil and a pinch of salt.

Ask your butcher to de-bone the quails for you so they are ready to grill. Barbecue, char-grill or sear quail in a very hot frying pan until they are medium rare – this should take 5–10 minutes; check them with a knife if you are not sure.

*Serves 4*

**To serve** *Remove from heat and let quail rest for a few minutes before drizzling with olive oil and serve with salsa.*

**Notes** *Peach salsa is also good with chicken thigh and lamb cutlets.*

*Barbecued quail is also great served on blanched beans (try a mixture of French, yellow and soy beans) that have been tossed with a dressing of sherry vinegar and a mix of walnut and extra-virgin olive oil.*

# Spatchcock with Crushed Garlic & BBQ Corn

4 spatchcock (poussin no. 5), boned

2 tbsp rosemary, chopped

4 cloves garlic

100 ml (3½ fl oz) extra-virgin olive oil

4 corn cobs, in leaves

2 tbsp butter

Put spatchcock in a bowl. Mix rosemary and garlic with the olive oil. Rub oil over the birds and leave to marinate for at least an hour before grilling.

**For the corn** Leave the husks on the corn and wrap each in two layers of foil. Put corn on the barbecue and cook for about 15–20 minutes, turning at intervals so corn will be cooked through. Alternatively, bake prepared cobs in an oven preheated to 200° (400°F) for about 30–40 minutes. Let corn rest while you cook the spatchcock.

Drain the majority of oil off the spatchcock, char-grill or barbecue each side for about 5–6 minutes, then set aside to rest.

*Serves 4*

*To serve* Serve a spatchcock per person, accompanied by a cob of corn coated in a generous amount of butter.

*Note* See pages 154–60 for some salads that would go well with this dish.

# Honey-roasted Chicken with Fennel & Mango Salad

100 ml (3½ fl oz) extra-virgin olive oil, plus extra to drizzle

1 tbsp honey

4 chicken fillets

1 large fennel bulb (or 2 smaller ones)

sea salt and freshly ground black pepper

40 g (1½ oz) flour

1 tbsp butter

1 ripe but firm mango, cut into 8 wedges, skinned

25 ml (1 fl oz) balsamic vinegar

60 ml (2 fl oz) chicken stock (see page 221)

handful of watercress for garnish

**For the chicken marinade** Mix together the extra-virgin olive oil and honey and marinate the chicken for 1–2 hours.

**Meanwhile, for the fennel** Wash the fennel well and slice very finely. Bring a saucepan of water to the boil, drop the fennel in for 1–2 minutes, then drain and refresh under cold water. Place the fennel in a bowl, drizzle with some extra-virgin olive oil and season well. Give it a good toss and set aside.

**For the chicken** Preheat the oven to 200ºC (400ºF). Dust the chicken fillets with flour. Heat a little extra-virgin olive oil in a frying pan and cook the chicken over a high heat until both sides are golden brown. Remove and place in the oven to finish cooking (about 5 minutes).

**Meanwhile, for the mango** In the same pan, add the butter and the mango, and cook for a few minutes until lightly coloured. Add the balsamic vinegar to the pan, then the chicken stock. Bring to the boil, then remove from heat.

*Serves 4*

**To serve** *Place some fennel in the middle of the plates. Place the chicken on top, the mango pieces on top of the chicken, drizzle with any mango pan juices and garnish with watercress.*

# Roasted Chicken Breast with Polenta, Leeks & Olives

4 free-range chicken breasts, skinless

2 leeks, white part only,
halved vertically

1 litre (2 pints) milk (or water)

200 g (6½ oz) instant polenta

200 g (6½ oz) parmesan, grated

sea salt and freshly ground
black pepper

4 tbsp kalamata or green olives, sliced

extra-virgin olive oil

**For the chicken** Preheat oven to
200°C (400°F). In a hot pan, sear
the chicken breasts on both sides,
transfer to an ovenproof dish and place
them in the oven to finish cooking
(about 8–10 minutes). Once chicken
is cooked, leave to rest in a warm
place. Blanch the leeks in boiling
salted water until soft. Set aside.

**For the polenta** Bring the milk or
water to the boil with a sprinkle
of salt and pour in the polenta in a
steady stream, stirring constantly.
Turn the heat down to very low and
stir until thick, about 5 minutes. Add
the parmesan and continue stirring
for a few minutes. Season well.

*Serves 4*

**To serve** *Spoon some polenta in the centre
of the plates. Slice the chicken breasts
on the diagonal and place on top. Top
with the leeks, sprinkle with olive slices
and drizzle with extra-virgin olive oil.*

# Tandoori Chicken with Curried Lentils & Cucumber Sour Cream

1½ tbsp tandoori paste or powder

100 g (3½ oz) natural yoghurt

4 chicken breasts, skin off

**Curried lentils**

30 g (1 oz) butter

1½ tbsp curry powder (buy a good blend or make up your own e.g. ground chilli, cumin, coriander, turmeric, fenugreek)

300 g (10 oz) green Puy lentils

**Cucumber sour cream**

1 large or 2 small continental cucumbers

250 ml (8 fl oz) sour cream

½ bunch mint, finely chopped

squeeze of lemon juice

sea salt and freshly ground black pepper

**For the chicken** Mix together the tandoori paste or powder, yoghurt and a pinch of salt and marinate the chicken in it for about 2 hours.

Preheat the oven to 180°C (350°F).

**For the lentils** Melt the butter in a medium saucepan and add the curry powder. Cook for about 20 seconds, then add the lentils, stirring until well coated. Add a generous pinch of salt. Cover with water and cook until tender, about 20 minutes. (Take care not to let the saucepan boil dry – you may need to top the lentils up with a little more water, but they shouldn't be too wet.)

**Meanwhile, for the cucumber sour cream** Halve the cucumber and scrape out the seeds with a spoon. Finely chop. Mix together the cucumber, sour cream, mint and lemon juice and season.

About 10 minutes before the lentils are ready, put the chicken in an ovenproof dish covered with foil. Bake for 10–15 minutes, depending on the size.

*Serves 4*

*To serve* Spoon some lentils on to a plate or plate/bowl, place the chicken on top, and spoon over a generous amount of the cucumber sour cream.

# Chicken & Veal Sausages with Tomato, Red Capsicum & Basil Compote

4 vine-ripened tomatoes, quartered

extra-virgin olive oil

sea salt and freshly ground black pepper

2 red capsicums

10 basil leaves, finely sliced

8 chicken and veal sausages (or veal, or chicken)

Preheat the oven to 200°C (400°F).

**For the compote** Sit the tomato quarters in a shallow ovenproof dish. Drizzle over a little extra-virgin olive oil, season, and roast until soft (about 25 minutes).

When the tomatoes are almost ready, cut the capsicums into large pieces as flat as possible. Lay them under the griller, skin-side up and very close to the flame, until the skin goes black and blistered (about 10 minutes). Put the pieces into a plastic bag and seal tightly. Leave for 5 minutes. Remove the capsicum from the bag and rub the blackened skin off with your fingers (it should come off very easily). Cut the flesh into fine strips.

Mix together the tomatoes, capsicum strips and basil.

**For the sausages** Grill the sausages to medium-rare, or as desired. Rest for a few minutes.

*Serves 4*

**To serve** *Place the compote in a small mound next to the sausages on each plate. Or, for a more rustic look, slice the sausages and toss with the compote, then serve on a large communal platter. Season well.*

# Salt-crusted Chicken with Artichoke Purée & Leeks

*The chicken is baked inside a salty dough, which is then thrown away, leaving the meat moist and tender.*

4 free-range chicken breasts

2 tbsp butter

2 large leeks, white part only, chopped

sea salt and freshly ground black pepper

extra-virgin olive oil

## Salt crust

410 g (14 oz) plain flour

125 g (4 oz) rock salt

1 tsp thyme

1 egg

170 ml (6 fl oz) water

## Artichoke purée

500 g (1 lb) Jerusalem artichokes, peeled

200 g (6½ oz) potatoes, peeled

500 ml (1 pint) milk

Preheat the oven to 200°C (400°F).

**For the salt crust** Mix together the flour, salt and thyme. Make a well in the centre, and add the egg and water. Stir together, then knead, to form a ball of dough. Wrap in clingfilm and place in the refrigerator.

**For the artichoke purée** Roughly chop the artichokes and potato. Cover with milk and add a little salt. Simmer for about 30 minutes or until soft. Drain most of the milk, but leave about 125 ml (4 fl oz) to help make a purée consistency. Keep warm.

**For the chicken** Roll out the dough to a thickness of about 5 mm (¼ in). Wrap up the chicken breasts, enclosing them within the pastry as best you can. If you don't have quite enough pastry, just wrap the pastry around the chicken as far as it will go and place the gap down on the baking tray. Place the fillets on a baking tray lined with baking paper and cook for 15 minutes. Remove from the oven and rest for 2–3 minutes.

While the chicken is resting, sauté the leeks in a pan with a little butter until soft. Purée the artichoke and potato mixture in a food processor. Add a knob of butter and season.

*Serves 4*

**To serve** Break open the salt crusts and discard. The chicken will have stayed steaming hot and moist inside. Slice each breast on the diagonal into 3 or 4 pieces. Spoon the purée onto serving plates to make a circle. Place the sliced chicken on top, arrange some leeks in a circle around the outside of the plate and drizzle with extra-virgin olive oil.

# Drunken Chicken with Dumplings

6 baby chicken (poussin, no. 5), boned

1 bunch asparagus (about 250 g/8 oz), peeled, sliced on bias into pieces 1 cm (½ in) long

500 ml (2 cups) chicken stock (see page 221)

100 g (3½ oz) polenta

50 g (1¾ oz) grated parmesan

20 g (1 tbsp) butter

3 tbsp chopped tarragon leaves

100 ml (3½ fl oz) Shaoxing rice wine

80 ml (2¾ fl oz) armagnac

extra 50 g (1¾ oz) butter

salt

## Dumplings

10 g (⅓ oz) pork back fat

1 egg

2 tbsp (about 20 g/⅔ oz) chopped sage

20 ml (1 tbsp) armagnac

sea salt

1 packet round gow gee wrappers

**For the dumplings** Separate the poussin thigh meat from breasts and mince thigh meat with the pork fat. Add egg, sage and armagnac. Season. Take out 1 sheet of wrapper pastry, place a spoonful of mixture in middle and fold sides up and around to make an open dumpling. Continue until mix is used up.

Blanch asparagus pieces, drain and set aside.

Heat chicken stock and add polenta. Bring to boil, then whisk in parmesan, butter and tarragon. Season. Add more stock if necessary to keep polenta at a pouring consistency.

Boil the Shaoxing wine with the 80 ml (2¾ fl oz) armagnac until reduced by two-thirds. Add the 50 g (1¾ fl oz) butter and season.

Steam dumplings for 10 minutes. While they cook, poach poussin breasts in the Shaoxing and armagnac sauce for 7 minutes, reserve sauce.

*Serves 6*

*To serve* Put a serving of polenta on each plate, scatter some asparagus around it, then place a poussin on top. Sit dumpling beside and pour sauce over.

# Spaghetti with Sesame-grilled Chicken, Carrot, Zucchini & Honey-mustard Butter

12 chicken thigh fillets

2 tbsp extra-virgin olive oil

2 tbsp honey

2 tbsp sesame seeds, toasted to golden brown in a saucepan

3 carrots

3 zucchini

500 g (1 lb) spaghetti

1 bunch coriander, chopped

**Honey-mustard butter**

100 g (6½ oz) butter, softened

1 tbsp honey

1 tbsp Dijon mustard

sea salt and freshly ground black pepper

**For the honey-mustard butter** Mix all ingredients together and refrigerate.

**For the marinade** Mix the extra-virgin olive oil, honey and half the sesame seeds together and marinate the chicken for 1–2 hours.

**For the spaghetti** Using a knife or a mandolin, slice the carrots and zucchini into long matchsticks, as long and fine as you can cut them.

Heat a large saucepan of salted water and add the spaghetti, cooking until al dente. A few minutes before it's ready, drop the carrots and zucchini into the same water to blanch.

**Meanwhile, for the chicken** Season the thighs and barbecue, char-grill or cook in a very hot frying pan until brown and glistening outside and just cooked through inside.

Strain the spaghetti and vegetables together, then tip it all back into the warm saucepan. Add a couple of tablespoons of mustard butter and a little extra-virgin olive oil, half of the chopped coriander and salt and pepper and toss through.

*Serves 4*

*To serve Put some spaghetti-vegetable mixture on each plate. Slice the chicken thighs into thick pieces on the diagonal and place on top of the spaghetti. Put a knob more mustard butter on top of the chicken and spaghetti to melt through, and sprinkle over remaining coriander and sesame seeds.*

# Poached Poussin with Polenta & Parmesan

4 poussin (no. 5 size), boned

100 g (3½ oz) rock salt

250 g (8 oz) duck fat

1 litre (1⅔ pt) chicken stock (see page 221)

100 g (3½ oz) polenta

150 g (5 oz) grated parmesan

sea salt and freshly ground black pepper

2 bunches (about 500 g/1 lb) asparagus, trimmed

1 bunch pencil leeks, trimmed

1 bunch (about 90 g/3 oz) tarragon, chopped

parmesan shavings

extra-virgin olive oil

Ask your butcher to bone the poussin, keeping the carcasses for stock (see page 219). Separate thighs from breasts.

Preheat oven to 100°C (215°F). Cover thighs with rock salt for 20 minutes then rinse off thoroughly. Place thighs in duck fat in an ovenproof dish and bake for 2 hours or until the meat flakes off the bone.

**For polenta** While the thighs are cooking heat 500 ml (1 pt) of stock in a heavy-based pan and whisk in polenta. Cook over low heat for 10 minutes, stirring constantly, then add the grated parmesan and continue to cook until polenta is ready – it will taste smooth and no longer grainy – approximately another 20 minutes. Season and set aside, keeping warm, until ready to serve.

**To poach breasts** Heat remaining chicken stock and slowly poach the poussin breasts until they are totally white and cooked – this will take about 5 minutes. Take breasts out of stock and rest.

While the breasts are poaching blanch the asparagus and leeks together in boiling, salted water. Mix the chopped tarragon into the polenta.

*Serves 6–8*

**To serve** *Place 1–2 thighs (depending on how large you would like the serve to be) in the centre of a plate. Put a spoonful of polenta over the poussin and place a little bit of the blanched vegetables on top of that. To finish, place a breast on top of the vegetables, and finally some long shavings of parmesan. Pour 2 tablespoons of the poaching stock over the top and drizzle with olive oil. Prepare the remainder of the plates in the same way.*

# Confit of Duck Leg with Bacon, Crushed Peas & a Mint Sauce

6 good-sized duck legs

500 g (1 lb) rock salt

2 kg (4 lb) tinned duck or goose fat

400 ml (13 fl oz) malt vinegar

100 g (3½ oz) brown sugar

1 bunch mint (about 60g/2 oz), leaves and stalks separated

12 rashers smoked pancetta

600 g (20 oz) frozen peas

butter

sea salt and freshly ground black pepper

**For confit** Rub duck legs with rock salt on both sides then place in a dish and cover with more salt. Place in fridge and leave for 2 hours.

Wash and pat duck legs dry with a towel. Place legs in a large ovenproof dish and completely cover legs with duck fat. Place in oven and cook on lowest setting – about 90–100°C (190–210°F) – for about 3–4 hours, or until the meat starts to come away from the bone. Remove from the oven and leave to cool down.

**For sauce** In a saucepan bring the vinegar and brown sugar to the boil. Once boiling add the mint stalks and allow to cool.

Carefully remove duck legs from fat once cool and place on a baking tray with 2 rashers of pancetta placed on top of each leg. Preheat oven to 180°C (350°F) and cook duck for about 20–25 minutes, until pancetta is slightly crisp and duck legs warm. While duck is heating place the defrosted peas in a food processor and roughly chop. Place peas in a pan with a good knob of butter, lots of seasoning and heat until hot.

Strain mint stalks from the vinegar, add roughly chopped mint leaves to the warm vinegar.

*Serves 6*

*To serve* Place a good spoonful of peas in the centre of each plate. Place duck leg on bed of peas, pour mint sauce over whole dish and serve with mashed potato (see page 166).

# Duck Breast with Szechuan Pepper, Pear & Turnip Salad

2 tbsp Szechuan peppercorns, ground or crushed in a pestle and mortar, plus extra 1 tsp

2 tbsp brown sugar

2 tbsp rock salt

4 small–medium duck breasts

1 turnip, peeled, finely sliced into half-moon shapes

250 g (8 oz) sugar

500 ml (1 pint) water

3 corella pears (or beurre bosc), cored, peeled and quartered

25 ml (1 fl oz) red wine vinegar

25 ml (1 fl oz) extra-virgin olive oil

pinch of sea salt

**For the marinade** Mix the crushed Szechuan peppercorns with the brown sugar and rock salt. Rub the duck breasts in the mixture until they are thickly coated on all sides.

Leave them to cure in the refrigerator for about 1 hour.

**Meanwhile, for the salad** Blanch the turnip in boiling salted water for 1–2 minutes. Remove and cool. Make a poaching liquid for the pears by heating the sugar with the water and stirring until the sugar has dissolved. Poach the pear quarters in the simmering liquid until soft, about 5 minutes. Remove.

Place 1 poached pear (4 quarters) in a food processor, along with the vinegar, extra-virgin olive oil, salt and about 1 tsp Szechuan pepper. Blend until smooth. Set aside to use as a dressing.

Slice the remaining 2 pears thinly and mix with the turnip. Toss the salad in some dressing, leaving a little to drizzle over the duck.

**For the duck** Preheat oven to 220ºC (425ºF). Place the breasts skin-side down in a frying pan over a low heat for 15–20 minutes. This melts off the fat and crisps the skin. Transfer to an ovenproof dish and finish cooking in the oven for about 5 minutes.

*Serves 4*

**To serve** *Place a small mound of salad on each plate. Slice the breasts and fan the pieces around the salad. Drizzle over some dressing.*

# Roast Duck with Honey & Clove Dressing

6 duck breasts

100 g (3½ oz) rock salt

100 g (3½ oz) brown sugar

100 ml (3½ fl oz) honey

100 ml (3½ fl oz) white wine vinegar

200 ml (7 fl oz) water

5 whole cloves

200 ml (7 fl oz) extra-virgin olive oil

Trim excess fat off the duck breasts and cover with equal quantities of sugar and salt, then cover with plastic film and refrigerate for 1 hour.

While the duck is curing make the dressing. Put honey, wine vinegar, water and cloves in a saucepan and boil until reduced by half. Chill, strain and whisk in olive oil.

**To cook the duck** Preheat oven to 180°C (350°F). Wash duck and dry it. Seal breasts in a pan, skin side down, until skin is crispy – about 4 minutes. Put in an ovenproof dish and roast for another 5 minutes. Remove from oven and rest for a further 5 minutes.

*Serves 4–6*

**To serve** *Slice the breast and spoon the dressing over the top.*

**Note** *The duck is good accompanied by noodles, a salad or Asian greens (see page 160).*

# Chicken & Tarragon Mayonnaise Sandwiches

250 ml (1 cup) chicken stock

2 free-range skinless chicken breasts

butter for spreading

16 slices white bread (e.g. Tip Top)

½ continental cucumber, thinly sliced

rocket for garnish

## Mayonnaise

2 free-range egg yolks

2 tsp Dijon mustard

2 tsp tarragon vinegar

200 ml (7 fl oz) extra-virgin olive oil

1 bunch (about 90g/3 oz)
tarragon, leaves finely chopped

sea salt and freshly ground
black pepper

Pour the chicken stock into a saucepan and add the chicken breasts. Bring to the boil, turn the heat down and simmer for about 5 minutes or until just cooked through. Leave the chicken to cool in the stock.

**To make the mayonnaise** Place the yolks, mustard and vinegar in a food processor and whiz until combined (or use a small bowl with an electric beater). With the motor running, gradually add the olive oil in a slow, constant stream until the mixture forms a mayonnaise consistency. Stir through the tarragon and season to taste. Makes about 250 ml (1 cup).

Butter the bread. Remove the chicken from the stock and slice thinly. Mix it with enough mayonnaise to bind. Make sandwiches with a layer of cucumber and a generous amount of chicken filling. Leave on the crusts and slice into three fingers. Serve garnished with rocket leaves.

*Makes 8 sandwiches*

# Meat Dishes

## Lamb, Beef & Pork

# Roast Lamb Rump with Tomatoes, Onion Confit & Basil Oil

4 oxheart tomatoes

100 g (3½ oz) rock salt

100 ml (3½ fl oz) extra-virgin olive oil

cracked black pepper

¼ bunch (about 30 g/1 oz) basil

4 spring lamb rumps
(120–150 g each/4–5 oz)

sea salt and freshly ground
black pepper

4 tablespoons onion confit
(see page 226)

Prick tomatoes with a skewer, halve them and place on a bed of rock salt skin side down. Drizzle with half the olive oil and sprinkle with black pepper. Bake in a low oven (100°C/215°F) for about 1 hour.

Chop basil and add it to the remaining olive oil, leaving it to infuse.

**To roast the meat** Preheat oven to 180°C (350°F). With a sharp knife score the fat side of the lamb rumps in a criss-cross pattern. Salt the meat and in a hot pan seal the meat: fat side down first, then the other side. Transfer to oven and cook for 8–10 minutes. Let meat rest for 5 minutes then slice it against the grain, cutting each rump into four pieces.

*Serves 4*

**To serve** Put 2 tomato halves on each plate, arrange the lamb slices over them and garnish with a tablespoon of onion confit. Drizzle the basil-infused oil over the top.

**Notes** The meat should be served medium-rare to medium.

Onion confit works with fish as well as meat: try poaching fish in equal quantities of wine and stock, then serve with steamed asparagus and a spoonful of onion confit finished with a drizzle of olive oil.

# Lamb Racks with Rosemary Crust & Garlic Purée

*Excellent with potatoes roasted in extra-virgin olive oil and rosemary.*

1 tbsp extra-virgin olive oil

4 lamb racks (3–4 chops per rack), trimmed of fat

sea salt and freshly ground black pepper

12 slices day-old white bread, crusts removed

leaves from 2 bunches rosemary

200 g (6½ oz) butter, melted

16 cloves garlic, skin left on

2 tbsp extra-virgin olive oil

Preheat the oven to 220°C (425°F).

**For the lamb racks** Heat the extra-virgin olive oil in a pan. Season the lamb racks and brown all over. Set aside.

**For the crust** Blend the bread and rosemary in a food processor until finely chopped and combined. Add the melted butter to bind and mix well. Using your hands, push the mixture on to the lamb racks evenly to a thickness of about 5 mm (¼ in).

Place in the oven with the garlic and cook for 10–12 minutes (for rare – longer if desired). Rest. Remove the garlic, cut the cloves in half and squeeze the soft contents into a small bowl. Add the extra-virgin olive oil and whisk together.

*Serves 4*

**To serve** *Spoon the garlic purée onto the plates and spread into a circle. Cut each rack into individual cutlets and place on the purée (don't worry if some of the crust comes off).*

# Lamb Fillets with Cabbage & Bacon, Star Anise Sauce

30 g (1 oz) butter

1 onion, finely sliced

180 g (6 oz) bacon, finely chopped

1 medium savoy cabbage, finely sliced

1 tbsp butter

1 tbsp extra-virgin olive oil

8 lamb fillets

250 ml (8 fl oz) veal or chicken stock (see pages 221, 222)

1 star anise, crushed in a pestle and mortar

a few drops of Pernod

a few chives for garnish, finely chopped

Preheat the oven to 220°C (425°F).

**For the vegetables** Heat the butter in a large saucepan. Add the onion and cook until soft. Add the bacon and cook a few minutes longer. Add the cabbage and mix well. Cook for 8–10 minutes, tossing well every now and then.

**Meanwhile, for the lamb** Heat the remaining butter and extra-virgin olive oil in a heavy-based frying pan and sear the lamb fillets until golden brown. Transfer to an ovenproof dish and finish cooking in the oven for about 3–4 minutes (for medium-rare).

**For the stock** In a small saucepan, add the stock, star anise and Pernod. Bring to the boil, simmer for 1 minute, then strain.

*Serves 4*

**To serve** *Spoon a mound of the cabbage mixture on each plate, top with 2 lamb fillets, drizzle over a little star anise sauce and garnish with chives.*

# Spicy Lamb With Basmati Rice, Green Olives & Preserved Lemon

800 g (1 lb 10 oz) lamb loin, milk-fed and trimmed of fat, or lamb fillets

4 tbsp panch phora spice blend

sea salt and freshly ground black pepper

1½ litres (3 pints) chicken stock (see page 219)

30 g (1 oz) butter

325 g (11 oz) basmati rice

1 tsp finely chopped preserved lemon

100 g (3½ oz) green olives, finely chopped

4 green (spring) onions, finely chopped

Preheat the oven to 250°C (475°F).

**For the panch phora** Buy the panch phora pre-mixed, or make your own using 3 parts brown mustard seed, 2 parts nigella seed, 2 parts cumin, 1 part whole fenugreek and 1 part fennel seeds.

Roll the lamb in the panch phora until it's well coated. Season well. Set aside.

**For the rice** Heat the chicken stock ready to ladle into the rice. In a large saucepan, melt the butter, add the rice and toss until well coated. Gradually add the hot stock by the ladleful, stirring constantly until rice is almost cooked (about 15 minutes) – you may not need to use all the stock. Add the preserved lemon and green olives; stir well.

**Meanwhile, for the lamb** Sauté the green onions in a pan with a little butter until soft. Remove and set aside. Turn the heat up and sear the lamb loin until well browned all over. Place in the hot oven for 10 minutes (for rare–medium, longer if preferred). Remove and rest for 5 minutes.

**Meanwhile, for the rice** Add a final ladleful of stock to the rice – it should be just tender but still quite moist, similar to risotto.

*Serves 4*

**To serve** *Divide the rice evenly among the serving plates. Cut the lamb on the diagonal into slices about 1 cm (½ in) thick, lay it over the rice and sprinkle the onions on top.*

# Roast Rack of Lamb with Oxheart Tomatoes, Radicchio & Asparagus

4 racks of lamb

4 cloves garlic, peeled and chopped

3–4 sprigs thyme

extra-virgin olive oil

4 oxheart tomatoes

sea salt and freshly ground
black pepper

2 bunches asparagus
(about 500 g/1 lb), trimmed

2 radicchio, quartered lengthwise

splash of balsamic vinegar

Trim the fat off racks, leaving some around the loins as protection. Marinate with slivers of garlic, thyme leaves and olive oil. Leave out at room temperature in marinade for an hour.

Preheat oven to 175ºC (345ºF). Cut tomatoes in half, season with salt and pepper and a little olive oil. Roast in oven for 20 minutes.

Seal lamb racks on all sides in a hot pan. Place in the oven for 5–6 minutes, then remove and allow to rest in a warm place for 10 minutes. While meat is relaxing, steam the asparagus until tender but still retaining some crispness. Put a little olive oil in a pan, heat and add the radicchio leaves; once they have wilted add a splash of balsamic vinegar to the pan.

*Serves 4*

**To serve** Put oxheart tomatoes in the centre of each plate. On top of tomatoes arrange a bed of radicchio. Carve the lamb racks into individual cutlets and place on the radicchio, drizzling the juices from the roasting pan over the top of the lamb. Arrange the asparagus around and on top of the lamb.

# Lamb Chops with Couscous & Mint Pesto

8 loin lamb chops, trimmed
of excess fat

1 tsp extra-virgin olive oil,
plus extra to drizzle

400 ml (12 fl oz) veal (or beef) stock
(see page 220)

150 g (5 oz) couscous

1 tbsp butter

**Mint pesto**

20 g (1 oz) English spinach

80 g (2½ oz) pine nuts

½ bunch mint, leaves only

extra-virgin olive oil

3 tbsp grated parmesan

sea salt and freshly ground
black pepper

Preheat the oven to 220°C (425°F).

**For the pesto** Blanch the spinach in
boiling water for 1 minute. Drain.

Toast the pine nuts in a pan over low
heat until lightly coloured. Remove.

In a food processor, blend the mint
leaves and spinach together with a little
extra-virgin olive oil. Add the parmesan
and pine nuts and blend to a smooth
paste. Add a little more extra-virgin
olive oil if required. Season. Set aside.

**For the lamb chops** Heat the oil in a
heavy pan and seal the chops, browning
them on both sides. Transfer to an
ovenproof dish and finish cooking
them in the oven (about 5 minutes).

Meanwhile, heat the stock. Put the
couscous in a saucepan and pour
on the hot stock. Put the lid on
and leave for a few minutes. Add a
knob of butter and fork through.

*Serves 4*

**To serve** *Spoon some couscous
on to serving plates, place 2 lamb
chops on top. Dollop a generous
spoonful of pesto over the chops.*

# Lamb Chops with Port & Red Wine Butter, & Rosemary Potatoes

250 ml (1 cup) port

250 ml (1 cup) red wine

1 red onion, finely chopped

250 g (8 oz) butter,
at room temperature

sea salt and
freshly ground black pepper

8 medium potatoes,
peeled and cut into 8 pieces

4 sprigs rosemary

extra 2 tbsp butter

1 tbsp extra-virgin olive oil

12 loin lamb chops

2 tbsp chopped parsley

**For the port and red wine butter**
Heat the port and red wine in
a small saucepan and simmer until
the liquid has reduced to about
⅓ cup (80 ml/2¾ fl oz). Cool
to room temperature.

Cook the red onion in 1 tablespoon
of the butter until soft. Cool.

In a small bowl, combine the
port/wine reduction and the rest of
the butter. Add the red onion. Beat
for 3–4 minutes, or until light and
fluffy. Season and keep in the fridge.

**For the potatoes** Cover the potatoes
with cold water, add one sprig of
rosemary and bring to the boil.
Immediately remove from heat and
strain. In a deep frying pan, heat the
extra butter and olive oil and sauté the
potatoes until tender inside and golden
brown and crisp on the outside (about
10 minutes). Just before potatoes are
ready, strip the leaves off the remaining
rosemary sprigs and add to the pan.

**Meanwhile** Grill (or barbecue)
the chops to your liking.

*Serves 4*

**To serve** *Serve chops on a bed of
potatoes, with a good dollop of red wine
butter on top. Garnish with parsley.*

# Lamb Burgers with Gruyère & Onion Confit

300 g (10 oz) lamb offcuts
(or lamb mince)

1 shallot

¼ bunch (about 30 g/1 oz) mint

1 egg

2 tsp sea salt

2 tsp dried chilli flakes

1 tbsp armagnac

30 ml (1 fl oz) oil

150 g (5 oz) gruyère

1 loaf Turkish bread

4 tbsp onion confit (see page 226)

Trim sinew and most of the fat from the lamb and mince in a food processor. Finely dice shallot and chop mint; add these to the mince. Add the egg, salt, chilli and armagnac.

Divide mix into 4 and roll into balls, then slightly squash down. Cook the burgers in a frying pan with a little oil (or on the barbecue) for 4 minutes on each side. Slice cheese into four and put a slice of cheese on each burger.

*Serves 4*

**To serve** Serve burgers on toasted Turkish bread with onion confit.

**Note** Onion confit (caramelised onions) can come in handy for all kinds of dishes, sandwiches and wraps.

# Veal Chops with Mum's Peas & Onion

4 rashers bacon, trimmed
of fat, thinly sliced

1 bunch spring onions,
whites only, finely chopped

185 g (6 oz) peas

400 ml (14 oz) veal or chicken
stock (see pages 221, 222)

1 tbsp extra-virgin olive oil

4 large veal chops

2 tbsp finely chopped parsley

In a pan, sauté the bacon rashers
until semi-crisp, add the onions
and cook until soft. Add the peas
and then the stock. Bring to the
boil. Season to taste. Keep hot.

Heat the extra-virgin olive oil
in a frying pan and cook the
chops until golden brown.

*Serves 4*

**To serve** *Place a chop on each
plate and spoon over the pea and
bacon mixture. Sprinkle with parsley
and serve with mashed potato.*

# Mum's Meatloaf

500 g (1 lb) minced steak

500 g (1 lb) sausage meat

2 rashers bacon, chopped

1 onion, chopped

60 ml (2 fl oz) HP Sauce

60 ml (2 fl oz) tomato sauce

1 tsp hot English mustard

½ bunch (about 60 g/2 oz) parsley

½ bunch (about 60 g/2 oz) marjoram

1 cup fresh breadcrumbs

1 tbsp sea salt

1 egg, beaten

Preheat oven to 150°C (300°F).

Mix meats together with bacon and
onion. Combine sauces with mustard
and add to meat. Chop herbs, add
to breadcrumbs with salt and add
to the mix. Bind together with the
beaten egg using your hands. Make
into a log roll and place on a baking
tray or mould into a loaf tin.

Bake in the oven for 1 hour.
Discard excess fat before serving,
and serve hot or cold.

*Serves 4–6*

**Note** *This recipe is very similar to
my mum's. We always ate it cold
on sandwiches the next day.*

# Steak & Kidney Pie

1 onion, peeled and diced

oil for cooking

4 rashers bacon, chopped

150 ml (5 fl oz) red wine

500 ml (2 cups) beef stock
(see page 222)

450 g (15 oz) sirloin steak

350 g (12 oz) lamb kidneys,
halved and trimmed

sea salt

flour for dusting

½ x 400 g (14 oz) can roma
tomatoes, roughly diced

freshly ground black pepper

½ bunch (about 75 g/2⅔ oz)
flat-leaf parsley

1 sheet puff pastry

Preheat oven to 200°C (400°F).

Gently soften onion in oil; when
soft add bacon and fry until
crispy. Add wine and heat until
reduced by half, then add beef
stock and reduce by half again.

While the stock reduces cut the steak
into 2 cm (¾ in) thick slices and
then in half; sprinkle with salt and
dust with a little flour. Quickly seal
meat in a hot pan in a little oil to give
it good colour but do not cook too
much. Salt, flour and seal kidneys.
Add both the kidneys and beef to the
bacon sauce with drained tomatoes
and heat until tomatoes are hot. Check
the seasoning and add the parsley.

Cut enough puff pastry to cover the pie
dish, put pastry on a greased baking
tray, make a cross in the top of the
pastry and cook in the hot oven until
golden brown – about 5–10 minutes.

*Serves 4–6*

**To serve** *Place hot mix in pie dish, put
pastry on top of pie dish and serve.*

**Notes** *It doesn't matter what size
or shape dish you use as long as
it is about 5 cm (2 in) deep.*

*The idea with this recipe is to cook
the beef for a very short time so it is
not tough. If you wanted to add other
vegetables you would use a cheaper
cut of meat and cook for longer.*

# Char-grilled Beef with Beef Ravioli & Turnip Purée

4 sirloin steaks

pinch of sea salt

extra-virgin olive oil

**Ravioli**

250 g (8 oz) braising beef (cheek, brisket or chuck steak)

250 ml (8 fl oz) red wine

¼ bunch thyme

1 clove garlic

sea salt and freshly ground black pepper

1½ litres (3 pints) veal or beef stock (see page 220)

1 tbsp butter

3 shiitake mushrooms, finely sliced

3 shallots, peeled and quartered

1 tbsp red wine vinegar

1 tbsp extra-virgin olive oil

1 packet gow gee wrappers

**Turnip purée**

2 medium turnips, peeled and sliced thinly

500 ml (1 pint) milk

**For the ravioli** Cut the beef into large dice. Marinate the meat in the red wine, thyme and garlic for about 12 hours. Remove the beef, but keep the liquid. Pour it into a small saucepan and simmer until reduced by half.

In a large saucepan over high heat, sauté the beef until golden brown and season. Pour the marinade over the beef, add the stock and braise for 2–3 hours, or until the beef is fall-apart tender. Remove the beef from the braising liquid. Set aside.

Melt the butter in a saucepan and sauté the mushrooms lightly. Remove. Add the shallots to the pan and cook in the butter gently until caramelised.

Mix together the beef, mushrooms and shallots. Whisk together the vinegar and extra-virgin olive oil and add to the beef mixture. Stir well to combine. Season.

Place about a dessertspoon of beef mixture onto a gow gee wrapper. Moisten the edges of the wrapper with water, fold it over into a half-moon shape and pinch the edges together firmly to seal. Repeat until all the mixture is used up. You should make about 12 ravioli.

**To make the turnip purée** Place the turnip slices in a saucepan, cover with milk, bring to the boil then simmer until soft. Drain and purée in a food processor.

Cook the steak in a hot frying pan or on a char-grill, to medium-rare, or as desired. Rest for a few minutes. Bring a large saucepan of salted water to the boil and blanch the ravioli to heat through. Remove with a slotted spoon.

*Serves 4*

**To serve** *Slice the beef in pieces about 5 mm (¼ in) thick, arrange on the plates next to some turnip purée topped with three ravioli per person. Sprinkle the beef with salt and drizzle over some extra-virgin olive oil.*

# Stir-fried Beef with Noodles

2 heads bok choy, cut in half lengthwise

2 tsp sesame oil

1 onion, sliced

2 cloves garlic, crushed

1 tbsp grated ginger

300 g (10 oz) beef fillet,
sliced into strips

1 red capsicum, sliced

100 ml (3½ fl oz) soy sauce

200 ml (7 fl oz) beef stock
(see page 222)

200 g (7 oz) dried somen
(Japanese) noodles

1 cup coriander sprigs

Blanch bok choy quickly in
salted boiling water and refresh
in iced water. Keep water boiling
to cook the noodles later.

Heat a wok with the sesame oil in it
until smoking stage. Fry the onion,
garlic and ginger, constantly stirring to
prevent them burning; add beef and
cook, stirring, until evenly coloured.
Add capsicum and continue to cook
for a further 3 minutes, add soy,
stock and bok choy and continue to
heat, tossing vegetables in sauce.

Cook the noodles in boiling
water, drain and add to the wok.
Continue cooking to reduce liquid.
Stir through coriander sprigs
and divide between bowls. Eat
straight away with chopsticks.

*Serves 4*

**Note** *You can substitute chicken
strips for the beef, but then use
chicken stock instead of beef stock.*

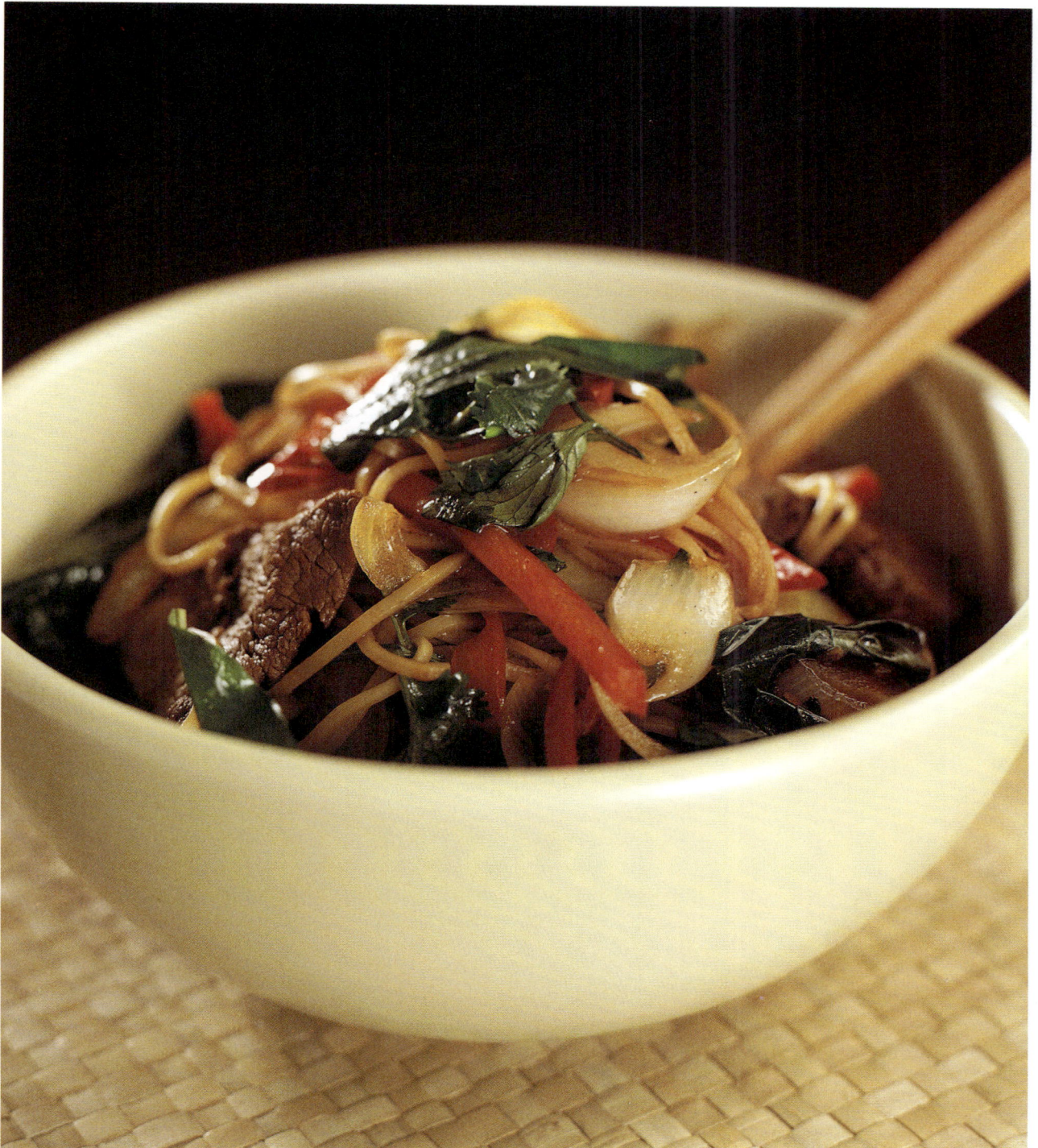

# Poached Fillet of Beef with Mushroom Custard & Caramelised Witlof

1.3 kg (2½ lb) beef fillet

sea salt

3 litres (5 pt) beef stock (see page 222)

handful of shiitake mushrooms, diced

### Caramelised witlof

75 g (2⅔ oz) butter

100 g (3½ oz) sugar

4 witlof, leaves halved lengthwise

100 ml (3½ fl oz) beef stock
(see page 220)

### Mushroom custard

500 g (1 lb) button mushrooms

100 g (3½ oz) shiitake mushrooms

1 tbsp butter

500 ml (1 pt) cream

pinch of salt

3 eggs

2 egg yolks

Trim any excess fat and white sinew strips from the beef fillet. Sprinkle with salt all over and seal in a hot pan so there is colour on all sides. Take out of the pan and rest until cool. When cool wrap in plastic film to create a tight cylinder and tie the ends. Chill in the fridge for 4 hours.

**For the custard** Quarter the mushrooms, wash well and drain. Melt butter in a pan and slowly cook the mushrooms until the water has evaporated. Add the cream and boil until liquid has reduced by a third. Season with salt. Blend and then strain the mix. Put in the fridge to chill. Mix the eggs and yolks together and add to the cold mushroom cream, tasting to check the seasoning: adjust if necessary.

Lightly oil six dariole moulds, and pour custard into them until they are half filled. Put moulds in a steamer and steam for 10 minutes. Let custards rest.

Bring beef stock to a rolling boil in large pan on the stove top. Unwrap beef, put it in the stock and cook for 15 minutes, making sure the stock boils continuously. Remove fillet and continue to boil the stock until it has reduced to one-third of its volume. Set sauce aside until ready to serve.

**To make the caramelised witlof** Melt butter and sugar in a saucepan over low heat, stirring, until sugar has dissolved and a light caramel has formed. Add witlof and stock and cook until the witlof has softened.

*Serves 6*

*__To serve__ Turn out the custards from moulds and put each on a dinner plate at 12 o'clock, then place a little bit of witlof on the right-hand side of the plate, and sliced beef on the left. Scatter a few shiitake mushrooms (blanched in the stock) over the plate and drizzle sauce around the outside.*

*__Note__ This recipe is ideal to serve at a dinner party. However, if you want to cook it for fewer than six people you can poach the beef in individual portions of 200 g (7 oz). Make sure the stock is not boiling in this case, just barely simmering.*

# Roast Rib of Beef with Spiced Beetroot

6 x 200 g (7 oz) scotch fillet steaks

1 tbsp butter

30 ml (1 fl oz) honey

250 g (8 oz) grated beetroot

½ tbsp sherry vinegar

sea salt and freshly ground
black pepper

**Spice mix**

10 g (½ tbsp) ground ginger

10 g (½ tbsp) ground cinnamon

10 g (½ tbsp) ground allspice

10 g (½ tbsp) ground nutmeg

Mix all spices together in a bowl.

**For the beetroot** In a heavy-based pot melt the butter then add the honey, stir to incorporate and then heat until the honey has caramalised lightly. Add 1 tablespoon of the spice mix, then add beetroot and cook until beetroot is soft but still crisp. Add vinegar and season with salt and pepper.

Preheat oven to 200ºC (400ºF). Sear all sides of steaks in a hot frying pan, then place in oven for 7–10 minutes. Rest beef above the oven or in a warm place for a further 10 minutes.

*Serves 6*

**To serve** *Slice beef and place on plates topped with spiced beetroot.*

# Roast Beef Fillet with Capsicum & Coriander

1 tbsp butter

1 tbsp extra-virgin olive oil

1 kg (2 lb) eye fillet of beef, in 1 piece

2 large red capsicums

1 bunch coriander

½ tbsp red wine vinegar

1 tbsp extra-virgin olive oil, plus extra to drizzle

sea salt and freshly ground black pepper

Preheat the oven to 200ºC (400ºC).

**For the beef** Melt the butter and oil together in a pan and cook the beef over a high heat, turning often, until lightly browned all over. Wrap in aluminium foil and bake for about 20 minutes (this is for medium-rare, but cooking time will vary depending on the thickness of the fillet). Rest the meat in the foil for 10 minutes.

**Meanwhile, for the capsicum** Cut the capsicums into large pieces as flat as possible, removing the seeds and core. Place the pieces under a hot griller, skin-side up, and close to the flame. Cook until the skin goes black and blistered (about 10 minutes). Put the pieces in a plastic bag and seal tightly. Leave for 5 minutes. Remove the capsicum and rub the blackened skin off with your fingers (it should come off very easily).

Finely chop the capsicum. Finely chop the coriander. Mix them together, add the vinegar and extra-virgin olive oil, season, and mix well.

*Serves 4*

**To serve** *When the beef is ready, serve in slices fanned around a small mound of capsicum salad. Drizzle the plate with a little more extra-virgin olive oil.*

# Grilled Sirloin with Tarragon Butter

300 g (10½ oz) field mushrooms

100 ml (3½ fl oz) extra-virgin olive oil

sea salt

freshly ground black pepper

30 ml (1 fl oz) white wine vinegar

¼ bunch (about 75 g/2⅔ oz)
flat-leaf parsley

4 x 200 g (7 oz) sirloin steaks

**Tarragon butter**

200 g (7 oz) butter, softened

30 ml (1 fl oz) honey

2 tbsp seeded mustard

½ bunch (about 45 g/1½ oz) tarragon

sea salt

**To make the tarragon butter** Process the butter in a food processor until very pale in colour, then add the honey and seeded mustard and process some more. Chop the tarragon leaves and add to the butter. Season with salt to taste. Scoop the butter on a rectangle of plastic film, roll up in the shape of a log, tie the ends like a bon bon and freeze. Once butter has set, store in the fridge.

Toss the mushrooms in oil, sprinkle with salt and pepper, and grill until soft and collapsed. When cooked put in a bowl and sprinkle with white wine vinegar. Chop parsley leaves and add to the mushrooms.

Grill the steaks for 4 minutes on both sides or until medium-rare and set aside to rest.

*Serves 4*

**To serve** Put a steak on each plate, slice the butter log into rounds and place 3 rounds on top of each steak. Serve grilled mushrooms on the side, with pieces of crusty bread.

**Note** This herb butter can also be served with fish and braised spinach, or simply spread on toasted sourdough bread.

# Fillet Steak Burgers with Aioli & Tomato Chutney

6 x 100 g (3½ oz) fillet steaks

sea salt

extra-virgin olive oil

6 sourdough bread rolls
or Turkish bread

1 bunch rocket (about 3 handfuls)

**Aioli**

2 large egg yolks

2 tsp white wine vinegar

1 tsp Dijon mustard

300 ml (10 fl oz) extra-virgin olive oil

1 clove garlic

sea salt and freshly ground
black pepper

**Tomato chutney**

1 kg (2 lb) second-grade tomatoes

2 onions, peeled

1 red capsicum

1 green apple

50 ml (1⅔ fl oz) extra-virgin olive oil

30 g (1 oz) mustard seeds

20 g (1 tbsp) curry powder

60 g (2 oz) brown sugar

150 ml (5 fl oz) malt vinegar

water

sea salt

**To make the chutney** Score the top of the tomatoes and blanch in boiling water. Refresh in iced water. Peel, cut flesh in half, squeeze seeds out and roughly chop. Dice the onion and capsicum; peel, core and dice the apple. Heat oil in a large pan then add onion and mustard seeds; cook until the seeds start to pop then add the curry powder, capsicum and apple. Add the tomatoes, sugar and vinegar, top up with water to cover vegetables and gently simmer, stirring occasionally, until chutney thickens – about 1½–2 hours. Season with salt.

**To make the aioli** Whisk egg yolks with vinegar and mustard, until yolk changes colour and thickens slightly. Slowly whisk in the oil until all is incorporated. Peel and crush garlic, then add, whisking to incorporate. If the aioli is too thick whisk in a little water to lighten. Season to taste.

Season steak with salt and cook on a barbecue or in a hot griddle pan for a few minutes on each side. Rest for 4 minutes, then drizzle with olive oil.

*Serves 6*

*To serve* Split the sourdough rolls in half. Spread the bottom of rolls with aioli, put a steak on top and then a dollop of chutney. Finish with a few rocket leaves and top with the other half of the roll.

*Notes* Any grilled bread can be used in this recipe instead of rolls: sourdough and Turkish bread are just as tasty.

Aioli can be used in BLTs and wraps, to accompany potato wedges, with seafood salad…the options are endless.

# Curried Sausages with Pilaf Rice

1 kg (2 lb) good quality beef sausages

½ large onion, peeled

2 carrots

vegetable oil

2 tbsp curry powder

2 x 400 ml (13 fl oz) cans coconut milk

150 g (5 oz) frozen peas

2 tsp sea salt

## Pilaf

200 g (1 cup) long-grain rice

5 g (1 tsp) butter

1 tsp saffron threads

1 tsp sea salt

1 tbsp white wine

625 ml (2½ cups) water

¼ bunch (about 30 g/1 oz) coriander

Preheat oven to 180°C (350°F).

**For the pilaf** Put all pilaf ingredients except coriander in an ovenproof dish and cover tightly with a lid or foil. Bake in oven for 30 minutes. When rice is cooked stir through chopped coriander.

**For the sausages** About halfway through cooking rice, bake sausages in the oven on a tray for 10 minutes. While the sausages are cooking, dice onion and carrot. Gently soften onion in a little oil in a pan, add curry powder and carrot and fry until aroma is released. Add coconut milk and simmer until carrot is tender.

When sausages are cooked drain the fat off, cut each into 4 slices and add to coconut curry. Add peas and simmer until they are cooked. Season and serve with pilaf.

*Serves 4–6*

*Notes* This recipe is the same as my mum's, but we never got pilaf because there were so many of us. We just got boiled long-grain rice and the amount she had to cook was huge.

*Curried sausages are spicier if reheated and eaten the next day.*

# Warm Pork Fillet Salad with Coconut Dressing

1 carrot

2 heads bok choy, chopped

100 g (3½ oz) bean shoots

250 g (8 oz) tofu

4 pork fillets

1 tsp cracked black pepper

1 tsp sea salt

juice of 2 limes

**Coconut dressing**

200 ml (5 fl oz) coconut milk

½ cup shredded coconut

75 ml (2½ fl oz) coconut cream

sea salt

**For the dressing** Bring coconut milk and shredded coconut to the boil together. Remove from heat, let cool and then chill slightly in refrigerator. Whisk or blend, slowly adding coconut cream as you do so, then season with salt.

Using a sharp peeler slice carrot into long ribbons. Blanch bok choy in boiling salted water then chill in iced water. Mix bok choy with carrot in a bowl with bean shoots and dress with a little of the dressing, just enough to coat the salad.

Cut tofu into 2 cm (¾ in) thick slices and then again into 2 cm (¾ in) batons. If you have a deep fryer (or large pot) heat oil to 180°C (350°F) and deep fry all slices until golden brown, then quickly put tofu in iced water, so the oil will separate from the tofu. If you don't have a deep fryer use a pan and shallow fry tofu one piece at a time, being careful not to let hot oil splash. Drain tofu.

Sprinkle pork with salt and pepper. Cook pork in a frying pan or on a hot barbecue for about 5–10 minutes, until slightly brown and cooked to medium. Rest fillets for a few minutes, then cut each into 4 pieces and squeeze lime juice over them.

*Serves 4*

*To serve* Mix tofu and fillets through salad and serve.

*Notes* Dressing can be kept refrigerated and used again for salads.

The dressing is also really good with fish if you add some fish stock to it (see page 221).

This salad is a good vegetarian dish if you leave out the pork.

# Soy-marinated Pork Chops with Coriander & Bean Sprouts

100 ml (3½ fl oz) honey

100 ml (3½ fl oz) soy sauce

4 pork chops (8 if they're small)

200 g (6½ oz) bean sprouts

sea salt and freshly ground
black pepper

1 bunch coriander, roughly chopped

**For the marinade** Mix together the honey and soy sauce and marinate the chops for 3–4 hours.

Preheat the oven to 220°C (425°F).

Remove the chops, saving the marinade. Pour the marinade into a small saucepan and simmer gently until it becomes a shiny syrup (about 5 minutes).

**Meanwhile, for the pork chops** Char-grill the chops or sear in a hot pan, then transfer to an ovenproof dish and finish cooking in the oven for a few minutes.

Blanch the sprouts in boiling salted water for a minute, then drain and season. Mix the coriander through the warm sprouts.

*Serves 4*

*To serve* Place the chops on plates with a small mound of sprouts next to them, and drizzle both with the hot marinade.

# Roast Pork with Spuds

2.5 kg (5 lb) pork leg, boned
and with skin on

150 g (5 oz) apricots (fresh
or dried organic)

150 g (5 oz) prunes

½ bunch (about 45 g/1½ oz) sage

100 g (3½ oz) toasted pine nuts

1 onion, peeled and diced

2 apples, grated

50 g (1¾ oz) butter, softened

sea salt and freshly ground
black pepper

### Roast spuds

6 desirée potatoes (about 1.5 kg/3 lb)

extra-virgin olive oil

sea salt

Preheat oven to 220°C (425°F).
Trim any excess fat and gristle
from the meat.

**To make the stuffing** Rip up apricots
and chop prunes and sage. Combine
these with pine nuts, onion, apple and
butter and season with salt and pepper.

With the tip of a sharp knife score
the pork skin all over at 2 cm (1 in)
intervals (to make the crackling). Turn
the meat over and along the long sides
of the piece separate the skin from the
meat (about 2 cm/1 in) and make
holes in the skin (with a sharp
knife) at regular intervals. Turn the
piece over so that the meat side is
facing up and spread stuffing over
the meat. Fold both long sides up
(like you are closing a book) and
tie by threading string through the
holes you created in the skin.

Put meat on a rack over a baking
tray. Salt skin liberally. If you have
any extra skin, score and salt that also,
and put it on another rack (to make
extra crackling). Put meat in oven and
allow to cook for 30 minutes per 500 g
(1 lb) meat.

**For the roast spuds** Peel potatoes
and cut into quarters. Put in saucepan
and cover with cold water. Bring
to boil and cook for 10 minutes or
until just tender. Strain potatoes and
return to the pan to evaporate all the
water, and toss gently to rough up
their edges. Drizzle with olive oil and
sprinkle with salt, put in a baking tray
and cook in oven towards the end of
the meat's cooking time until golden
brown – about 30–40 minutes.

Remove pork from oven and allow
to rest for at least 20 minutes
before serving.

*Serves 6–8*

**To serve** *Serve sliced, with stuffing on the
side, plenty of crackling and potatoes.*

# Salads & Vegetables

# Asparagus, Snowpea Sprout & Orange Salad

2 oranges

50 ml (1½ fl oz) extra-virgin olive oil

sea salt and freshly ground
black pepper

16 asparagus spears,
woody ends trimmed

½ punnet snowpea sprouts,
ends trimmed

**For the oranges** Cut the skin off the orange with a knife, cutting away the pith too. Cut into segments, removing pips as you go.

**For the dressing** Squeeze any orange juice from discarded pith and skin into a little bowl, then whisk in the extra-virgin olive oil. If you don't have enough juice, take 1 of the segments and squeeze the juice in. Season and set aside.

**For the asparagus** In a saucepan of boiling salted water, blanch the asparagus, then refresh in cold water. Cut into halves or thirds.

*Serves 4*

*To serve* Mix the asparagus with the orange and snowpea sprouts, add the dressing and toss well. Serve in one large bowl or on individual plates.

# Radicchio & Orange Salad

1 radicchio

3 oranges

**Dressing**

50 ml (2½ tbsp) extra-virgin olive oil

50 ml (2½ tbsp) balsamic vinegar

sea salt and freshly ground
black pepper

Remove the outer leaves and stalk of the radicchio. Cut into quarters and soak in water until ready to serve.

Drain and dry the leaves. Peel the oranges using a knife, cutting away all the white pith as well. Cut each into about 8 segments.

Whisk the vinegar and olive oil together. Season to taste. Toss the radicchio and orange segments in the dressing. Serve immediately.

*Serves 4*

**Note** *The bitterness of the radicchio is balanced by the sweetness of the orange and balsamic. You could also use witlof.*

# Mushroom & Bean Sprout Salad

200 g (7 oz) button mushrooms, sliced

250 g (8 oz) bean sprouts

1 punnet (about 90 g/3 oz) mustard cress or alfalfa and radish sprouts

**Dressing**

1 tsp Dijon mustard

50 ml (1⅔ fl oz) cider vinegar

125 ml (½ cup) extra-virgin olive oil

sea salt and freshly ground
black pepper

For the dressing, whisk together the mustard, vinegar and olive oil and season to taste.

Combine the mushrooms, bean sprouts and mustard cress or alfalfa. Toss with the dressing and serve.

*Serves 6*

**Notes** *Good when served with leftover roast pork or turkey.*

*You can also use different varieties of mushrooms, such as oyster, shiitake and enoki.*

# Bean Salad with Pine Nuts & Currants

1½ tbsp currants, soaked in port

50 g (1½ oz) pine nuts

12 snake beans, topped, tailed and cut to the same length as the other beans

12 French beans, topped and tailed

12 Roman beans, topped and tailed

**Dressing**

25 ml (1 fl oz) cider vinegar

50 ml (1½ fl oz) hazelnut oil

squeeze of lemon juice

**For the currants** Put the currants in a shallow bowl and pour on enough port to just cover them. Leave to soak overnight.

**For the pine nuts** In a pan, toss the pine nuts over medium heat until lightly browned.

**For the beans** Bring a large saucepan of salted water to the boil. Add the snake beans and cook for 1 minute; add the remaining beans to the pan and cook for a further 1½ minutes. Refresh in iced water and drain.

*Serves 4*

**To serve** *Place the beans in a bowl and sprinkle over the currants and pine nuts. Whisk the vinegar, oil and lemon juice together, pour over the beans and toss well. Serve in a deep bowl.*

# Snowpea & Chilli Salad with Almonds

400 g (14 oz) snowpeas

1 small red chilli, de-seeded
and finely chopped

50 g (1¾ oz) slivered almonds, toasted

½ bunch (about 45 g/1½ oz)
coriander, roughly chopped

**Dressing**

2 tbsp hoisin sauce

2 tbsp red wine vinegar

80 ml (2¾ fl oz) extra-virgin olive oil

sea salt and freshly ground
black pepper

To make the dressing, whisk
together the hoisin sauce, vinegar
and olive oil. Season to taste.

Top, tail and de-string the snowpeas.
Blanch in boiling water for about
15 seconds then drop into iced
water. Drain and combine with
the chilli, almonds and coriander.
Toss with the dressing and serve.

*Serves 6*

*Notes This makes a good summer
lunch served with ham off the
bone and Warm Potato Salad.*

# Warm Potato Salad

1 kg (2 lb) new potatoes

**Dressing**

25 g (1 tbsp, heaped) Dijon mustard

20 ml (1 tbsp) red wine vinegar

250 ml (1 cup) extra-virgin olive oil

sea salt and fresh ground black pepper

¼ bunch (about 15 g/½ oz) chives

Put potatoes into a pan of cold,
salted water and bring to boil.
Cook until potatoes are soft when
tested with a knife, but do not
allow them to become mushy.

While potatoes are cooking combine
mustard and vinegar. Slowly add
oil, whisking vigorously. Check for
seasoning. Drain potatoes, cut in
half and when slightly warm toss
them in the dressing and chives.

*Serves 4–6*

*Notes If you add dressing to the
potatoes when they are too hot the
dressing will separate: it won't look
as good, but it will still taste fine.*

*Other combinations for potato salad:*

*1 When the potatoes are still warm toss
with rocket, lemon juice and olive oil, then
season with salt and serve immediately.*

*2 Cut potatoes in half and toss with pesto.*

# Daikon Radish & Rocket Salad

1 medium daikon radish

2 tsp butter

2 tsp honey

2 tsp sesame seeds

sea salt and freshly ground
black pepper

100 ml (3½ fl oz) mirin

1 bunch rocket

extra-virgin olive oil

Using a potato peeler, cut the radish
into ribbons all about the same size.
In a medium saucepan, melt the
butter and honey together to form a
light caramel sauce. Add the sesame
seeds, a splash of water, then the
radish ribbons. Season lightly, cover
and cook for a few minutes, until the
radish is al dente. Drain and let cool.

In a small saucepan, simmer the
mirin for a few minutes until
it reduces slightly. Cool.

*Serves 4*

**To serve** *Using your hands, mix
the radish with the rocket. Drizzle
with mirin and extra-virgin
olive oil, season and serve.*

**Note** *This salad is excellent served
with prawns or smoked salmon
for a light starter or lunch.*

# Asian Greens

30 ml (1 fl oz) extra-virgin olive oil

2 tsp ginger, grated

2 kaffir lime leaves, chopped

200 g (7 oz) shiitake mushrooms, sliced

½ Chinese cabbage, shredded

15 ml (1⅔ fl oz) fish stock
(see page 221)

Heat oil in a large frying pan,
add shallot, ginger, lime leaves and
mushrooms. Add cabbage and saute for
3 minutes, add the fish sauce and stock
and simmer until cabbage collapses.

*Serves 4*

**Notes** *If you can't find the fresh shiitake
mushrooms, you can use the dried ones,
just follow the instructions for rehydration.*

*You can also use any other green
Asian vegetables. Others too that
go nicely are spinach, broccolini
or even beans and snowpeas.*

# Grilled Baby Corn, Fetta & Pear Salad with Walnut Dressing

2 tbsp sherry vinegar

4 tbsp walnut oil

1 tbsp extra-virgin olive oil

pinch of sea salt

2 bunches rocket

80 g (3 oz) good quality fetta

1 ripe beurre bosc pear, cut into 12 thin wedges

12 pieces baby corn

**For the dressing** Shake or whisk together the vinegar, walnut oil and extra-virgin olive oil and add a pinch of salt.

**For the salad** Put the rocket leaves in a large bowl and pour in half the dressing. Mix well with your hands. On each serving plate, place some rocket leaves, piling them up to give a little height.

Crumble the fetta and sprinkle on top of the rocket. Arrange three pear wedges on top of each pile.

**Meanwhile, for the baby corn** Char-grill, or toss in a very hot, heavy frying pan until slightly coloured.

*Serves 4*

**To serve** *Place the baby corn between the pear slices on the salad. Drizzle with remaining dressing.*

# Cauliflower & Almonds with Parmesan

1 cauliflower

75 g (2⅔ oz) butter

75 g (2⅔ oz) slivered almonds

75 g (2⅔ oz) grated parmesan

2 tbsp chopped chives

Divide cauliflower in florets. Bring pan of salted water to the boil and cook cauliflower for 3–4 minutes, until tender. Drain well. Put the butter and almonds in a heavy-based pan, heat to melt butter then add florets. Gently mix, then sprinkle in the parmesan. To serve, garnish with chopped chives.

*Serves 4–6*

# Beans & Shallots

250 g (8 oz) green beans, topped and tailed

1 tbsp butter

1 shallot, chopped

Cook beans in boiling salted water for 2 minutes. Drain well. Put butter in a heavy based pan with shallot, cook for a minute, then add beans and toss together before serving.

*Serves 4–6*

# Sautéed Field Mushrooms with Parsley & Onion

100 g (3½ oz) unsalted butter

1 small onion, finely chopped

6 large field mushrooms,
cut into eighths

pinch of sea salt

4 tbsp finely chopped flat-leaf parsley

In a large frying pan, melt the butter.
Add the onion and cook until soft.
Add the mushrooms and sauté over
medium heat for a few minutes. Season
well with salt and sprinkle in three-
quarters of the parsley. Mix gently.

*Serves 4*

**To serve** *Sprinkle remaining
parsley over the mushrooms.*

# Brussels Sprouts with Bacon

500 g (1 lb) brussels sprouts

100 g (3½ oz) bacon, chopped

1 tbsp butter

Remove any loose leaves from the
sprouts and using a small knife make
a criss-cross cut in each base. Bring
a pan of salted water to the boil, add
sprouts and boil for 4 minutes, then
drain very well. Put sprouts, bacon and
butter in a heavy-based pan and cook
until bacon starts to crisp up slightly.

*Serves 4–6*

# Mashed Potatoes

4 large potatoes, peeled and quartered

2 tbsp butter

100 ml (3½ fl oz) cream

sea salt and freshly ground
black pepper

extra-virgin olive oil

1 tbsp finely chopped chives

Run cold water over the potatoes
for about 10 minutes to remove any
starch. Put them in a large saucepan,
cover with water and add a good
pinch of sea salt. Bring to the boil
and simmer for about 20 minutes, or
until soft. Drain and push through
a mouli. Refrigerate until cold.

Once cold, push through a fine sieve,
and put in a saucepan over low heat.
Add butter and cream and stir together
until potato is hot. Season to taste.

*Serves 4*

**To serve** *Put in a large serving
bowl, drizzle with olive oil
and sprinkle with chives.*

# Rosemary Potatoes

8 medium potatoes,
peeled and cut into 8 pieces

4 sprigs rosemary

2 tbsp butter

1 tbsp extra-virgin olive oil

Cover the potatoes with cold water,
add a sprig of rosemary and bring to
the boil. Remove from heat and strain.

In a deep frying pan, heat the butter
and olive oil and sauté the potatoes
until tender inside and golden brown
and crisp on the outside (about 10
minutes). Just before they are ready,
strip the leaves off the remaining
rosemary sprigs and add to the pan.

*Serves 4*

**Note** *You can leave the potatoes
whole, but increase the cooking time.*

# Colcannon

500 g (1 lb) potatoes, peeled

2 tbsp butter

125 ml (4 fl oz) warm milk

250 g (8 oz) cabbage, finely chopped

1 tbsp butter

1 tbsp water

1 large onion, finely chopped

2 tbsp butter

2 tbsp parsley, finely chopped

sea salt and freshly ground
black pepper

**For the potatoes** Bring a large saucepan of salted water to the boil and cook the potatoes until soft. Drain and mash with the 2 tbsp butter and warm milk.

**For the cabbage** In another saucepan, add the tablespoon of butter, water and cabbage, toss well and cook over a very gentle heat with the lid on until tender.

Melt the 2 tbsp of butter in a frying pan and add the onion, cooking until soft.

*Serves 4*

*To serve* Add the cabbage, onion and parsley to the mashed potato and stir until well combined. Season and serve hot.

# Desserts & Sweet Things

# Figs in a Bag

**Per person**

2 small figs

10 g (½ tbsp) butter

30 ml (1 fl oz) muscat
(sweet white wine)

1 tbsp brown sugar

2 tsp smashed hazelnuts

1 tbsp mascarpone

Score the top of the figs and stuff butter down into their middle. Toss the figs in the wine, sugar and nuts. Cut a square of greaseproof paper and place the figs in the middle, pull the sides up and tie with twine.

Preheat oven to 180°C (350°F) then bake bag or bags for 10–15 minutes or until the outside of the paper goes a little bit brown.

*To serve* Cut the top of the bag and dollop mascarpone on top of the figs. If you want to serve on a plate cut off the top and pour figs into a bowl to retain the juices before adding mascarpone.

*Notes* This is a simple dessert that can be prepared in advance and cooked just before you want to eat.

*The juices and the mascarpone should ooze together. Yum!*

*The bags can be cooked on a barbecue, over low heat – put them on after you have finished cooking the main course.*

# Grilled Fruit with Mascarpone

2 nectarines

2 white peaches

2 peaches

2 mangoes

10 leaves Vietnamese mint

200 g (7 oz) mascarpone

Halve and stone the nectarines and peaches. Slice the cheeks of the mangoes and use a sharp knife to make a criss-cross pattern in the flesh down to the skin.

Grill fruit under a hot griller (or barbecue): put the fruit flesh side down, cook for 4 minutes and then turn over and cook another 4 minutes, or until the fruit starts to caramelise.

*Serves 4*

*To serve* When fruit has caramelised put a quarter of the fruit on each person's plate, sprinkle with shredded mint and dollop with mascarpone.

*Notes* Most fruits can be grilled and will go a nice golden colour because of their sugar content. Check what fruit is in season.

*You can also cook the fruit in a pan and splash with Grand Marnier when almost cooked.*

# Grilled Figs with Port Syrup & Mint

250 ml (8 fl oz) port

½ bunch mint, leaves only

3 medium-sized figs, trimmed and cut into quarters

3½ tbsp icing sugar

clotted cream to serve

Pour the port into a small saucepan. Add the mint leaves (keep a few to slice finely for garnish), and simmer until the port has a slightly syrupy consistency (about 5 minutes). Strain to remove the mint leaves.

Place the figs in a shallow dish and pour the strained port over them. Leave for half an hour.

Remove the figs with a slotted spoon (keep the port), sprinkle with icing sugar and place under the griller until the sugar caramelises and turns golden brown.

*Serves 4*

**To serve** *Place 3 fig pieces in each shallow bowl, spoon over some port syrup, dollop on some clotted cream and sprinkle with sliced mint leaves.*

# Blood Oranges Poached in Sangria

4 blood oranges (6 if they're small)

1 cup caster sugar

1 cinnamon stick, broken in half

3 cloves, lightly crushed

250 ml (1 cup) dry red wine

200 ml (7 fl oz) port

50 ml (1⅔ fl oz) Cointreau (optional)

mascarpone, to serve

chopped mint, to garnish

Preheat the oven to 180°C (350°F).

Using a potato peeler, cut three 6 cm (2 in) lengths of peel from one of the oranges and set aside. Peel all the blood oranges using a knife, cutting away all the white pith as well as skin. Roll oranges in the sugar and place in a baking dish, tipping any excess sugar into the dish, along with the strips of peel, cinnamon stick, cloves, wine, port and Cointreau.

Bring to the boil on the stove, stirring the liquid a little. Turn the oranges over, cover and place in the oven for 10 minutes, turning the oranges once, halfway through.

Remove from oven and let cool.

When the oranges are cool, place in a smaller container so that they are fully submerged in the liquid and refrigerate overnight.

*Serves 4*

**To serve** *Slice the oranges into rounds, spoon over some syrup and top with a dollop of mascarpone and a sprinkle of mint.*

**Note** *Navel oranges work just as well in this recipe. You can also just drink the sangria with ice.*

# Strawberries & Grapes Marinated in Champagne, Mint & Lemon

2 punnets strawberries

200 g (7 oz) seedless black grapes

500 ml (2 cups) champagne (or sparkling wine), plus a splash extra

250 g (1 cup) caster sugar

zest of 1 lemon

½ bunch (about 75 g/2⅔ oz) mint, leaves torn

500 ml (2 cups) water

Hull the strawberries and halve them if big. Pick the grapes off the stalks and place in a large bowl with the strawberries.

In a saucepan, bring the champagne, sugar, lemon zest, mint and water to the boil, stirring to dissolve the sugar. Turn the heat down and simmer for 5 minutes. Pour the liquid over the fruit and cover with plastic film to seal in the flavours.

*Serves 6–8*

*To serve* Once cool, serve in martini glasses with a splash of extra chilled champagne on top. (Drink any leftover liquid!)

*Note* You could use different berries and liquids – maybe peach schnapps and sparkling water.

# Strawberry Gratin

2 punnets strawberries, washed and hulled

2 eggs

50 g (1¾ oz) caster sugar

100 ml (3½ fl oz) champagne or sparkling wine

Divide the strawberries (about 10 per person) into individual gratin dishes or shallow serving bowls that will fit under the griller.

In a small saucepan over very gentle heat – or a stainless-steel bowl inside a larger saucepan of gently simmering water – whisk the eggs, sugar and bubbly together until they turn pale and fluffy (2–3 minutes). Gently pour the mixture over the strawberries and place under a griller until the top goes golden brown (or colour with a blowtorch). Serve immediately.

*Serves 4*

# Baked Berry Tart

1 quantity sweet pastry (see page 220)

250 g (8 oz) almonds

250 g (8 oz) butter

250 g (8 oz) caster sugar

60 g (2 oz) plain flour

3 eggs

1 tsp Grand Marnier

100 g (3½ oz) blueberries

100 g (3½ oz) blackberries

100 g (3½ oz) raspberries

Preheat oven to 150°C (300°F). Roll out pastry and line a flan dish about 30 cm (12 in) in diameter. Put a circle of greaseproof paper on the pastry base, cover with rice and blind bake for 15 minutes, until lightly golden brown. Remove from oven and discard rice and paper. Increase oven heat to 160°C (320°F).

Pulse almonds in the food processor until fine. Take almonds out and pulse butter and sugar together until pale and creamy, then add almonds and pulse until combined. Transfer mix to a bowl and sift in flour. Beat eggs and slowly add to the mix. Finally add Grand Marnier.

Fill tart case almost to the top with mixture and poke berries all through it. Bake for approximately 25 minutes or until golden brown on top.

*Serves 6–10*

*Notes* *If you chill the tart before serving it is easier to cut.*

*You could substitute peaches or pears for the berries: just cut these fruits into eighths and arrange in tart so there is enough fruit in each slice.*

*The mix does rise a bit, so don't overfill.*

*Leftover mix can be kept in the fridge for a day or two and used in another dish.*

# Poached Pears in Red Wine

150 g (5 oz) caster sugar

500 ml (2 cups/1 pt) red wine

4 pears (such as beurre bosc
or Williams), peeled

2 cinnamon sticks

200 g (7 oz) clotted or double cream

In a pan mix sugar into the wine, and gently heat until sugar has dissolved. Put the pears in this liquid, add enough water to cover the pears and throw in cinnamon sticks. Gently simmer until the pears are soft and a knife goes through them easily (make sure they aren't too soft because they will continue to cook while cooling).

Core pears and let them sit in the wine until cold. Pour some of the liquid into another pan and heat until it has reduced to a syrup consistency.

*Serves 4*

**To serve** *Put a dollop of cream in a bowl and place a pear on top, then drizzle with syrup.*

**Note** *This is best served warm. The pears can be poached well in advance and reheated, making this a great dessert for a dinner party.*

# Fresh Fruit Jelly with Dessert Wine

250 g (8 oz) stone fruits (e.g. peaches, apricots, cherries, plums), peeled and stones removed, roughly chopped

150 ml (5 fl oz) water

125 g (4 oz) caster sugar

rind of 1 lemon (cut in one spiral)

200 ml (6½ fl oz) sweet dessert wine

50 ml (1½ fl oz) lemon juice, strained

1 tbsp gelatine

extra fresh fruit and cream (optional)

In a saucepan, place the fruit, water, sugar and lemon rind. Bring to the boil, stirring to dissolve the sugar. When boiling, remove from heat and take out the rind. In a food processor, purée the fruit and syrup, then strain through a fine sieve. If you want to make the jelly very clear, you can pass the liquid through filter paper inside muslin, but it's not essential.

You should have about 350 ml (11½ fl oz) of purée. Stir in the dessert wine and lemon juice. Heat a little of the liquid and stir in the gelatine until dissolved, then mix into the rest of the liquid. Pour into individual moulds (about 85 ml/3 fl oz) or 1 large mould and refrigerate overnight to set.

*Serves 6–8*

**To serve** *Dip moulds into hot water for a few seconds to turn out the jelly. Serve with fresh fruit and lightly whipped cream.*

# Lemon Tart

*This is a creamy tart that uses lime and orange juice, as well as lemon juice.*

## Pastry

250 g (8 oz) plain flour

90 g (3 oz) icing sugar

125 g (4 oz) butter, cubed

rind of ½ lemon, grated

½ vanilla bean, seeds only

1 egg

butter and dusting flour, for greasing

handful of dried beans or rice

## Filling

5 eggs

200 g (6½ oz) caster sugar

rind of ½ lemon, grated,
and juice of 1 lemon

rind of ½ lime, grated,
and juice of 1 lime

rind of ½ orange, grated,
and juice of 1 orange

125 ml (4 fl oz) cream

1 tbsp icing sugar (optional)

Preheat the oven to 180°C (350°F).

**To make the pastry** Sieve the flour and icing sugar into a large bowl. Gradually add the cubes of butter and rub in with your fingers (or place the flour, icing sugar and butter in a food processor and blend until it resembles breadcrumbs). Make a well in the centre, and add the lemon rind and vanilla seeds. Beat the egg and pour into the well. Stir a little with a wooden spoon, then use your hands to mix together, kneading well until it all comes together in one ball. Wrap it in plastic film and place in the refrigerator for 30 minutes.

Grease a 26–28 cm (10½–11 in) tart mould with removable base, then dust it with flour and tip out the excess.

Roll out the pastry on a floured surface to a size big enough to line the flan tin and overhang the sides a little. Lay the dough on top of the tin and gently ease it in with your fingers. Trim the excess around the top with a sharp knife. Refrigerate for a further 30 minutes.

Blind bake the case by laying a piece of greaseproof in the pastry and weighing it down with a few dried beans or rice. Bake for 10 minutes, then remove the beans and paper and bake for a further 10 minutes, or until lightly golden and cooked through.

**For the filling** Whisk the eggs with the sugar and rind of the lemon, lime and orange. Stir in the juices and fold in the cream. Pour the filling into a jug.

Turn the oven down to 120°C (250°F). Slowly pour the filling into the hot pastry case (this ensures that the pastry case will be sealed). Bake for 30–40 minutes, or until just set. (It should be wobbly but not runny when you touch the centre lightly with your finger.) Remove from the oven. Cool.

**Option** To give the tart a nice caramelised top, sieve the extra icing sugar on top and place it under a hot griller until it browns and bubbles.

*Serves 6–8*

# Lemon Sunshine Pudding

1 tbsp plain flour

250 g (8 oz) sugar

1½ tsp grated lemon rind

4 tbsp lemon juice

4 free-range eggs, separated

250 ml (8 fl oz) milk

pinch of sea salt

Preheat the oven to 180°C (350°F).

Combine the flour, sugar, lemon rind and juice, lightly beaten egg yolks and milk and mix well. In another bowl, beat the egg whites with the salt until stiff. Fold into the lemon mixture.

Pour into a shallow, greased, ovenproof dish. Sit the dish in a pan of hot water to come halfway up the sides. Bake for 45–50 minutes. The pudding will have a very soft sponge top and a lemon sauce underneath.

*Serves 4–6*

# Quince Charlotte

1 kg (2 lb) quinces, peeled

40 g (1½ oz) clarified butter
(see page 223)

60 g (2 oz) caster sugar

40 ml (1½ fl oz) calvados (optional)

pinch of ground cinnamon

## Charlotte mould

2 tbsp unsalted butter

30 g (1 oz) caster sugar

17 thin slices white bread,
crusts removed

150 g (5 oz) clarified butter
(see page 223)

**For the charlotte mould** Grease the charlotte tin well with the unsalted butter, then pour in the caster sugar, shaking it around until it clings to the base and sides of the tin. Tip out the excess.

Cut 8 slices of bread in halves diagonally, 7 slices in halves vertically and leave 2 slices whole.

Brush 8 bread triangles (you will need the remaining 8 later) with some clarified butter and lay them in the base of the tin, points in the centre, overlapping each other with no gaps. Brush the 14 rectangular halves with clarified butter and line them vertically around the sides of the tin, overlapping slightly and leaving no gaps. They should come up to the top of the tin.

Preheat the oven to 180°C (350°F).

**For the quinces** To prepare the quinces, quarter them, remove the cores, then cut the quarters in half again. The quinces should be cooked in 2 batches.

Pour half the clarified butter into a large, heavy, non-stick pan, add half the sugar and melt until a caramel has formed. Add half the quinces and sauté, stirring and tossing, until they are well coated and slightly coloured (about 5 minutes). Watch out you don't get burnt by spitting caramel.

Add a pinch of cinnamon and deglaze with half the calvados. Remove the quinces, and repeat the process with the remaining butter, sugar, quinces, cinnamon and calvados.

Place half the quinces in the mould, pouring over a little of the caramel juices. Top with the 2 whole slices of bread. Place the remaining quinces on top, again pouring over a little of the caramel juices. Brush the remaining 8 bread triangles with clarified butter and layer them on top, points in the centre and slightly overlapping to leave no gaps. Cover with a piece of buttered foil and bake for 1 hour, or until quinces are tender when you test with a skewer.

Remove from the oven and rest in the tin for 1 hour.

*Serves 6–8*

**To serve** *Invert the charlotte on to a serving plate by placing the plate over the top of the tin and turning the tin and plate upside-down. Cut into wedges and serve warm with cream.*

# Sweet-wine Custard

100 ml (3½ fl oz) sweet dessert wine

130 ml (4 fl oz) Granny Smith
apple juice, strained

350 ml (11½ fl oz) cream

2 free-range eggs

7 egg yolks

75 g (2½ oz) caster sugar

3 tbsp icing sugar

Preheat the oven to 130°C (275°F).

In a small saucepan, simmer the
dessert wine until it reduces by
half. Add the apple juice to the
wine and heat to a simmer.

Pour the cream into another small
saucepan. Heat to a simmer.

In a bowl, whisk the eggs, yolks and
caster sugar until just combined.
Pour the hot cream on to the egg
mixture, whisking constantly, then
add the wine/apple juice liquid,
and whisk well until combined.

Pour through a strainer into a
jug, then into ramekins about
125 ml (4 fl oz) capacity.

Place the moulds in a baking dish and
pour in hot water to come a third of
the way up the moulds. Bake for 50
minutes, or until the top feels firm
and the custard has just set. Remove
from the oven, cool and refrigerate.

*Serves 6*

**To serve** *Sprinkle icing sugar on top
and place under a hot griller until the
top caramelises, like a brulée. Serve
with almond tuile or cat's tongue.*

# Chocolate & Mint Pots

200 g (7 oz) good-quality
dark chocolate

300 ml (10 fl oz) cream

¼ bunch (about 30 g/1 oz) mint

1 gelatine sheet

2 eggs

100 g (3½ oz) caster sugar

1 sheet puff pastry

icing sugar (for dusting)

Roughly chop chocolate and melt in a pan over a bain marie. Bring half the cream to the boil with the leaves from the mint. While the cream is heating soften gelatine in cold water. Take the cream off the heat and add the gelatine (discard water).

Whisk eggs and sugar together in a bowl over another bain marie until light in colour and doubled in size (like a sabayon). Remove from heat and either continue whisking by hand or use an electric mixer and whisk until cold. Fold gelatine cream into chocolate and quickly pass through a sieve. Fold whisked eggs into chocolate mixture.

Semi-whip remaining cream and fold through the whole mix. Pipe out into little pots (small espresso cups would be excellent) and refrigerate.

Preheat oven to 210°C (410°F). Cut puff pastry into 1.5 cm x 10 cm (½ in x 4 in) strips and twist from both ends. Place on a tray, sprinkle with icing sugar and bake in oven for 5 minutes or until golden brown.

*Makes 10 small pots*

*To serve* Serve the chocolate pots with the pastry sticks on the sides.

*Note* Work as fast as you can when handling puff pastry. It is best to do so on a chilled bench as the pastry will quickly heat up the more you handle it, and will then be hard to twist. To chill a bench fill a baking tray with ice and cold water and put tray on the bench for a few minutes: the bench will cool down and will be a suitable surface for working with pastry.

# Chocolate & Date Cake

50 g (1½ oz) dried dates,
roughly chopped

2 tbsp armagnac or any brandy

350 g (11½ oz) dark chocolate
(couverture is best), roughly chopped

150 g (5 oz) unsalted butter,
chopped into cubes

125 g (4 oz) caster sugar,
plus extra 75 g (2½ oz)

60 ml (2 fl oz) strong espresso coffee

50 g (1½ oz) self-raising flour, sieved

4 tbsp cocoa, sieved

4 eggs, separated

Soak dates in armagnac for 1 hour.

Preheat the oven to 180°C (350°F).
Grease a 20 cm (8 in) square cake
tin with a removable base. Line
the base with baking paper.

Heat the chocolate, butter, 125 g sugar
and coffee in a small saucepan inside
a larger saucepan of gently simmering
water, stirring until completely melted
and shiny. Remove from heat. Fold
the flour and cocoa into the hot
chocolate mixture, and transfer to a
mixing bowl. Whisk the yolks and
add to the mixture. Add the dates
in the armagnac and mix well.

Using an electric mixer or whisk,
beat the egg whites, gradually adding
the extra sugar, until soft peaks
form. Gently fold the whites into the
chocolate mixture, pour into the cake
tin and bake for 1 hour, or until the
top is firm but the centre remains soft
and moist. Cool completely in tin.

*To serve* Dust the cake with cocoa
*and serve with lightly whipped*
*cream (you can also add chopped*
*dried dates or a little armagnac*
*– or both – to the whipped cream).*

# White Chocolate Mousse with Berries

400 ml (14 fl oz) cream

2 free-range eggs

250 g (8 oz) white chocolate (couverture)

1 tsp gelatine

1 tbsp boiling water

300 g (10 oz) fresh berries (e.g. strawberries, blueberries, blackberries)

Beat the cream until semi-whipped, without being too stiff. Set aside.

In a small saucepan inside a larger saucepan of very gently simmering water, whisk the eggs until frothy and pale; remove from heat and continue whisking until cool. The eggs should be creamy – if they have cooked too quickly they will be lumpy and almost like scrambled eggs (throw them away and start again!).

In another small pan, melt the chocolate over very gentle heat. Dissolve the gelatine in 1 tbsp of boiling water.

Pour a third of the egg mixture into the chocolate and stir well, then fold in the remaining egg mixture. Add the semi-whipped cream and the gelatine and stir until well combined.

Leave in the refrigerator for 4 hours or overnight to set.

*Serves 4*

**To serve** *Spoon the mousse onto serving plates and surround with fresh berries.*

# Chocolate Brûlée

6 egg yolks

100 g (3½ oz) caster sugar

400 ml (13 fl oz) cream

70 ml (2⅓ fl oz) milk

125 g (4 oz) dark chocolate, finely chopped

In a large bowl whisk the egg yolks with sugar until combined. Bring cream and milk to the boil together and immediately pour into the egg mixture. Return to saucepan and heat gently, stirring constantly, and cook until the custard coats the back of a wooden spoon. Add chocolate and stir until it has dissolved. Pour into brûlée moulds. Chill in fridge to set for about 2–3 hours before serving.

*Serves 6*

# Citrus, Almond & Polenta Cake

525 g (1 lb 4 oz) caster sugar

5 free-range eggs

2 egg yolks

500 g (1 lb) almond meal

50 g (1½ oz) polenta

1 tsp baking powder

juice and rind of 1 orange, finely grated

juice and rind of 1 lime, finely grated

juice and rind of 1 lemon, finely grated

butter for greasing the tin

3 tbsp icing sugar for dusting

mascarpone (optional)

fresh berries for serving (optional)

Preheat the oven to 150ºC (300ºF).

Grease a 25 cm (10 in) tin with removable base (or springform tin), and line the base with baking paper.

In a large mixing bowl, beat the sugar, eggs and yolks until pale and fluffy. Stir in the almond meal, polenta and baking powder. Mix well. Strain the juices and add to the bowl along with the grated rind and mix well until thoroughly combined.

Pour the cake mixture into the tin and bake for 1 hour and 15 minutes. The top should have a firm crust, and inside should remain moist (but not wet) when tested with a skewer. Leave to cool in the tin.

**To serve** Dust with icing sugar and serve with mascarpone and fresh berries (optional).

# Baked Lemon Cheesecake

250 g (8 oz) packet Scotch Finger
(or other plain, sweet) biscuits

80 g (2½ oz) melted butter

500 g (1 lb) cream cheese

60 g (2 oz) caster sugar

1 tsp vanilla essence

3 free-range eggs

2 egg yolks

375 ml (12 fl oz) cream

juice and rind of 1 lemon

50 g (1½ oz) plain flour

**For the base** Crush the biscuits well and mix with the melted butter. Grease a springform tin about 20–25 cm (8–10 in) diameter and, using your fingers, press the mixture to evenly cover the base and sides of the tin. Refrigerate for 15 minutes.

Preheat the oven to 150°C (300°F).

For the filling Mix all the remaining ingredients together and beat until smooth and creamy. Pour into the biscuit base and bake for 40 minutes, or until the top is firm to touch.

*Serves 10–12*

*Note This cheesecake is light and cheesy, not too sweet.*

# Apricot Ricotta Cake

butter and raw sugar for
greasing the cake tin

75 g (2½ oz) caster sugar

7 free-range eggs, separated

500 g (1 lb) ricotta cheese

juice and rind of 3 oranges

125 g (4 oz) plain flour

200 g (6½ oz) dried apricots, chopped

3 tbsp flaked almonds

icing sugar for dusting

Preheat the oven to 180°C (350°F). Grease a 20 cm (8 in) cake tin with butter and sprinkle over some raw sugar, tipping out the excess.

Beat the caster sugar and egg yolks until pale. Fold through the ricotta, orange rind and juice, flour and apricots. Whisk or beat the egg whites to soft peaks and fold into the mixture.

Pour into the cake tin, sprinkle with flaked almonds and bake for 1 hour. Let the cake cool in the tin for 10 minutes before turning out.

*To serve Dust with icing sugar and serve with crème fraiche.*

# Pavlova with Fresh Berries & Mascarpone

1 tsp olive oil

4 free-range egg whites

150 g (5 oz) caster sugar

1 tsp white wine vinegar

1 tbsp hot water

200 g (6½ oz) mascarpone

300 g (10 oz) mixed berries
(e.g. raspberries, blackberries,
blueberries, loganberries)

icing sugar to dust

Preheat the oven to 150°C (300°F).
Cut a piece of greaseproof baking
paper to fit on to a flat oven
tray and brush with the oil.

Beat the egg whites, sugar, vinegar
and hot water together until soft
peaks form. Using a spatula or knife,
shape the whites into a 20 cm (8 in)
round on the baking tray, or into
4–6 individual rounds if you prefer.

Bake in the middle of the oven for
1 hour and 10 minutes (about 1 hour
for individual pavlovas) until crisp
on the outside but marshmallowy
on the inside. Cool on a wire rack.

*Serves 4–6*

**To serve** *Spread the mascarpone thinly
on to the centre of the pavlova, pile the
berries on top and dust with icing sugar.*

# My Version of Mum's Trifle

**Sponge**

125 g (4 oz) sugar

4 eggs

100 g (3½ oz) flour

25 g (¾ oz) butter, melted

**Jelly**

1 punnet raspberries

1 punnet blueberries

½ punnet strawberries

3 sheets gelatine

400 ml (13 fl oz) sugar syrup
(see page 226)

**Crème pâtissière**

500 ml (2 cups) milk

1 vanilla bean, halved vertically and
seeds scraped out

6 egg yolks

125 g (4 oz) sugar

40 g (1½ oz) cornflour

icing sugar

100 ml (3½ fl oz) strawberry liqueur

200 ml (7 fl oz) cream, whipped

grated dark chocolate

**For the sponge** Preheat oven to 190ºC (375ºF). Whisk sugar and eggs together in beater until doubled in size and light and fluffy. Then slowly sieve in flour, folding gradually through the mix. When the flour has been incorporated, gently stir through melted butter. Grease 1–2 rectangular baking trays (depending on size of trays) and pour mix out on to the trays. Bake in oven for 8–10 minutes: when cooked sponge should be golden brown.

**To make crème pâtissière** Put milk in pan and add vanilla bean and seeds; bring close to boil and then set aside, for milk to infuse. Whisk eggs and sugar together until pale and ribbon-like, sift cornflour in and mix thoroughly. Remove vanilla bean from milk and slowly whisk milk into the egg mix, then return all to the pan. On low heat stir until the mix bubbles; once bubbling cook for 4 minutes, stirring, or until flour taste has gone. Transfer to a bowl, sprinkle with icing sugar and refrigerate.

**To make the jelly** Halve strawberries and scatter on the bottom of a large casserole dish with the other berries. Dissolve the gelatine in a small amount of water then heat sugar syrup and pour over gelatine. Cool jelly mixture slightly before pouring over berries.

**To assemble the trifle** Put a sheet of sponge over the jelly and cut to size. Brush with strawberry liqueur until sponge is soaked through. Refrigerate until set. When ready to serve mix crème pâtissière with whipped cream and spread on top. Sprinkle with grated chocolate.

*Notes* You can use the crème pâtissière in any other recipe that requires custard, such as pastry tarts.

*Use the same proportion of gelatine to liquid to make your own individual jellies.*

# Peach Clafoutis with Amaretto

unsalted butter and plain flour for greasing a 23 cm (9 in) flan dish

500 g (1 lb) fresh peaches, ripe but firm (or canned peaches)

50 g (1½ oz) caster sugar

50 ml (1½ fl oz) water

juice of ¼ lemon

icing sugar for dusting

**Batter**

100 ml (3½ fl oz) milk

½ vanilla bean, split vertically

150 ml (5 fl oz) cream

60 ml (2 fl oz) Amaretto liqueur

4 eggs

120 g (4 oz) caster sugar

pinch of sea salt

25 g (1 oz) plain flour

Preheat the oven to 180°C (350°F). Grease a 23 cm (9 in) flan dish with butter and dust with flour. Tip out the excess.

**For the peaches** Peel the peaches if you want to, or leave the skin on. Cut the peaches in half and remove stones. In a large saucepan or frying pan, heat the sugar, water and lemon juice, stirring until the sugar is dissolved. Add the peach halves, cut side down. Cover and cook for about 3 minutes. Turn the peaches over and cook for a further 3 minutes. Remove from the heat and allow peaches to cool in the covered pan. (If using canned peaches, simply drain them, then make the batter.)

**For the batter** In a small saucepan bring the milk and vanilla bean to the boil. Remove from the heat and leave for 5 minutes to allow the vanilla flavour to infuse. Discard the vanilla bean. Add the cream and Amaretto to the milk. Set aside.

In a bowl, whisk the eggs, sugar and salt until pale and fluffy. Fold in the flour and pour the milk mixture in through a fine strainer or sieve. Mix well.

Arrange the peach halves, cut side down, in the flan dish and gently pour over the batter. Bake for 30–35 minutes, or until just set.

*Serves 6–8*

**To serve** Serve warm, dusted with icing sugar.

# Apple & Rhubarb Crumble

**Crumble**

150 g (5 oz) butter

150 g (5 oz) plain flour

150 g (5 oz) roasted hazelnuts

150 g (5 oz) caster sugar

**Stewed rhubarb and apple**

4 sticks rhubarb

4 green cooking apples

50 g (1¾ oz) caster sugar

100 ml (3½ fl oz) water

**For the crumble topping** Soften butter and pulse in a food processor with flour, nuts and sugar until breadcrumb consistency. Spread out on a tray and bake in a moderate oven (180°C/350°F) until golden brown. Let the crumble cool down completely. Break up the crumble and keep in a sealed container until you are ready to serve.

**For the stewed rhubarb and apple** Wash rhubarb and cut into 5 cm (2 in) long pieces. Peel, core and cut apple into eighths. Put the fruit into separate saucepans and cover each with half the sugar and water. Cut pieces of greaseproof paper to fit over the fruit and cook on medium heat until the fruit is cooked but still slightly firm (the apple may take longer then the rhubarb).

*Serves 6 (with leftovers)*

*To serve* Mix the apple and rhubarb together and place in a warm serving dish. Sprinkle with crumble and serve while still warm with a dollop of ice-cream.

*Notes* Everyone loves crumble. To make it easier if you are busy, the fruit can be stewed beforehand and then warmed through when ready to serve.

*My trademark crumble topping never fails, it's always a winner!*

# Pear Tart with Mascarpone

4 individual sweet pastry tart cases (see page 220), or one large tart case

handful of dried beans or rice

3 pears, peeled, halved, cored and seeded

750 ml (1½ pints) water

250 g (8 oz) sugar

juice of ½ lime

½ vanilla bean, split vertically

2 free-range eggs, separated

1 egg yolk

60 g (2 oz) caster sugar

250 g (8 oz) mascarpone

3 tbsp icing sugar

liqueur (e.g. Amaretto, cognac, schnapps)

Preaheat oven to 200°C (400°F)

**For the pastry cases** Roll out the dough and, using your fingers, ease it into the greased tart moulds (either 10 cm/4 in tartlet cases or 1 large mould). Trim the excess pastry around the top with a sharp knife. Refrigerate for 30 minutes. Blind bake the pastry cases by cutting pieces of baking paper to sit inside the cases and adding some dried beans or rice. Bake for about 7 minutes, then remove the beans and paper and bake for a further 5–10 minutes, until golden and cooked through. Cool.

**For the pears** Poach the pear halves by bringing the water, sugar, lime juice and vanilla bean to the boil, stirring to ensure the sugar has dissolved. Add the pears and simmer until soft (about 5 minutes). Remove and set aside.

**For the mascarpone** In a small saucepan inside a larger saucepan of gently simmering water, whisk the egg yolks with the caster sugar until they turn pale and fluffy. Remove from heat and continue whisking until the mixture cools slightly. Slowly whisk in the mascarpone.

In a separate bowl, beat the 2 egg whites until soft peaks form. Fold the mascarpone mixture into the egg whites.

Serves 4

**To serve** *Spread the mascarpone cream into the tarts. Cut each pear half in half again, dust with icing sugar and place under the griller for a couple of minutes until the sugar caramelises and the pears colour a little. Lay the pear pieces on top of the mascarpone cream and drizzle a little liqueur on and around the tarts.*

# Bread & Butter Pudding with Marsala Crème Anglaise

**Marsala crème anglaise**

3 free-range egg yolks

60 g (2 oz) caster sugar

250 ml (8 fl oz) milk

½ vanilla bean, split vertically

1 tbsp Marsala

**Pudding**

200 g (6½ oz) unsalted butter, melted

8–10 slices white bread,
cut in halves diagonally

300 ml (10 fl oz) milk

300 ml (10 fl oz) cream

pinch of salt

1 vanilla bean, split vertically

5 free-range eggs

3 tbsp caster sugar

4 tbsp sultanas

**For the Marsala anglaise** Whisk the egg yolks with the sugar in a bowl. In a small saucepan, bring the milk and vanilla bean to the boil. Remove the vanilla bean and pour the hot milk into the egg yolk mixture, whisking well, then return the mixture to the hot saucepan. Over a gentle heat, stir constantly, until the mixture thickens enough to coat the back of a spoon. Remove from the heat and strain into a jug or bowl. Cool. Add Marsala to taste, about a tablespoon, and stir in. Refrigerate until needed.

**For the pudding** Preheat the oven to 140°C (275°F). Grease a baking dish, about 25 cm (10 in) in diameter and about 5 cm (2 in) deep. Dip the bread into the melted butter, coating both sides, and place in the dish, overlapping the triangles so that they cover the base.

Bring the milk, cream, salt and vanilla bean to the boil. Remove from heat and discard vanilla bean. Whisk the eggs and sugar together and add to the milk mixture, whisking well.

Pour the custard over the bread slices and sprinkle the sultanas on top. Bake for about 1 hour, or until the custard is set.

*Serves 6–8*

***To serve*** *Serve warm, in generous portions, with the Marsala crème anglaise.*

# Lemon Meringue Tartlets

200 g (7 oz) sweet pastry (see page 218)

**Filling**

125 g (4 oz) butter

5 eggs

145 g (5 oz) caster sugar

2½ lemons

**Meringue**

175 g (6 oz) caster sugar

35 ml (1 fl oz) water

20 ml (1 tbsp) glucose

3 egg whites

Defrost pastry if needed and roll out very thinly on a chilled and floured workbench (see Notes). Roll pastry back onto the pin and lay over greased mini muffin tins. Using a small amount of pastry dipped in flour, mould pastry into muffin tin, then prick pastry bases. Put in the freezer for 15 minutes to prevent shrinking in the cooking process. While pastry chills preheat oven to 180°C (350°F). Cook tartlets in oven for 8–10 minutes or until golden brown. Let cool and set aside.

**To make filling** Dice butter, melt in a medium saucepan and then let it cool slightly. Beat eggs with sugar and add juice of lemons and zest of one lemon. Add to butter and cook over medium heat, stirring constantly until thick. Don't worry about any lumps because they will disappear later. Blend with hand-held mixer, strain and chill. Store in a piping bag until ready to serve.

**To make meringue** Boil sugar, water, and glucose together until it reaches 110°C (225°F) – at this stage it should start forming a brittle thread when pulled with a fork. While sugar is heating, beat egg whites in mixer until stiff. Slowly add sugar mix to egg whites and beat until cool and shiny.

**To serve** Pipe lemon mix into the bottom of pastry cases, then pipe meringue on top of lemon mix and either put under a preheated, very hot griller or use a blowtorch to caramelise.

**Notes** To chill a bench, fill a baking tray with ice and cold water and put tray on the bench for a few minutes: the bench will cool down and will be a suitable surface for working with pastry.

This recipe can be adapted to produce a large tart for a dinner party or a family meal: use a large fluted pastry flan case, and serve each slice with some cream and fresh raspberries.

The shells and curd can be made well in advance and just put together before serving.

This is also nice without the meringue.

# Mango & Coconut Bombe

## Jocande sponge

6 egg yolks

120 g (4 oz) caster sugar

50 g (1¾ oz) butter, melted

100 g (3½ oz) plain flour

50 g (1¾ oz) cornflour

7 egg whites

130 g (4 oz) caster sugar

## Coconut ice-cream

375 ml (12½ fl oz) cream

175 ml (6 fl oz) milk

25 ml (¾ fl oz) Malibu

100 g (3½ oz) coconut, toasted

85 g (2¾ oz) coconut sugar, coarsely grated

3 egg yolks

## Mango sorbet

12 g (⅓ oz) glucose

65 ml (2¼ fl oz) sugar syrup (see page 226)

250 ml (1 cup) mango purée, passed through fine sieve

1 tsp ginger juice, strained

25 ml (¾ fl oz) lime juice, strained

## Italian meringue

6 egg whites

50 g (1¾ oz) caster sugar

extra 180 g (6 oz) caster sugar

40 ml (1⅓ fl oz) hot water

50 g (1¾ oz) shredded coconut

**For the sponge** Preheat oven to 160ºC (320ºF). Whisk egg yolks and the 120 g (4 oz) sugar together until pale. Fold in melted butter. Sift the flours and fold through mixture. Whisk egg whites until frothy and add 130 g (4 oz) sugar to the whites in a steady stream, whisking constantly until stiff peaks form. Fold the whites into the yolk and flour mix, pour into a greased, flat tray (standard slice tray) and cook in oven for 5–7 minutes.

**To make the coconut ice cream** Bring cream, milk, Malibu, toasted coconut and coconut sugar slowly to the boil, stirring regularly to prevent sugar and coconut scorching. Remove from heat and stand to let flavours develop for 30 minutes. Lightly beat yolks then return coconut cream to the heat and bring to the boil; pour cream on to yolks and return mixture to saucepan. On low heat and stirring constantly, cook until the mix thickens and will cover the back of a wooden spoon. Strain through a very fine-meshed sieve (ideally a chinois) into a bowl over ice. When cool churn in an ice-cream maker until firm.

**To make the sorbet** Dissolve glucose in sugar syrup, then combine all ingredients and churn in ice-cream maker until frozen and smooth in texture.

**To make the meringue** Whisk egg whites to a soft peak. Add the 50 g (1¾ oz) sugar and whisk until combined. Meanwhile, put remaining 180 g (6 oz) sugar in a small pan with hot water and stir to dissolve. Bring to boil, cook to 120ºC (245ºF) (firmball stage – a drop of syrup put into cold water will form a firm ball), then remove from heat. Add syrup to egg whites and beat until mix is cooled.

**To make the bombes** Slice sponge into 3 mm (¼ in) thickness or as thin as possible. Line the inside of 6 Chinese teacups – or similar shaped dishes. Spoon in coconut ice cream until the teacups are half full. Then fill the rest with mango sorbet and place a circle of jocande sponge on top, so bombe is entirely enclosed. Put in freezer for 1 hour or until completely frozen.

Preheat oven to 190–200ºC (375–390ºF). Run a knife around the sides of each teacup and turn out sponges – the top will now become the bottom. Place on a baking tray lined with baking paper. With a palette knife, cover sponge with a thin layer of meringue, making sure that it is entirely covered with meringue. Flick the meringue to resemble spikes and cover with shredded coconut. Place in oven for 3–5 minutes or until lightly golden brown. Serve immediately.

*Serves 6*

# Iced Mango Parfait

1 large mango

300 ml (10 fl oz) cream

3 free-range eggs

2 egg yolks

175 g (6 oz) caster sugar

1 tbsp Cointreau

Peel the mango and slice the flesh off the stone. Purée the flesh in a food processor – you should have about 200 ml (6½ fl oz). Set aside.

Beat the cream until stiff peaks form. Set aside.

In a small saucepan inside a larger saucepan of gently simmering water, whisk the eggs, yolks, sugar and Cointreau until they turn pale and fluffy. Whisk constantly, and continue whisking for a few minutes after you've removed the mixture from the heat as it cools down.

Add the mango purée to the whipped cream, then add the egg mixture. Mix well.

Pour into a loaf-shaped 9 cm x 19 cm (3½ in x 7½ in) tin lined with clingfilm and freeze overnight.

*Serves 6–8*

**To serve** *Lift the frozen parfait out of the tin and cut into thick slices. Serve with fresh mango or strawberries on the side (optional).*

# Lavender, Maple & Almond Bavarois with Poire William Sauce

5 leaves gelatine

5 egg yolks

50 g (1¾ oz) caster sugar

1 litre (1⅔ pt) milk

200 ml (7 fl oz) cream

300 ml (10 fl oz) maple syrup

12 lavender stalks (blossom only)

300 g (10½ oz) toasted almond flakes

2 pears, peeled, halved and cored, cut into 0.5 cm (¼ in) cubes

## Sauce

100 ml (3½ fl oz) Poire William

100 ml (3½ fl oz) water

100 ml (3½ fl oz) sugar syrup (see page 226)

Put gelatine leaves in cold water to soften.

Whisk the egg yolks and sugar together until combined. Set aside.

Bring milk, cream, maple syrup, lavender and almonds to the boil in a saucepan and simmer for 5 minutes. With a Bamix or hand-held mixer blend together.

Strain lavender cream over egg-yolk mixture. Squeeze excess moisture from gelatine and whisk into hot mixture. Return to clean saucepan and cook over low heat, stirring continually, until the cream thickens enough to coat the back of a spoon.

Lightly oil 6 dariole moulds and pour mixture in them up to the brim. Refrigerate and allow to set overnight – at least 12 hours.

**For the sauce** Combine all ingredients.

*Serves 6*

*To serve Dip moulds in hot water to loosen bavarois. Turn out onto plates, add diced pear and surround with sauce.*

# Licorice Parfait with Lime Syrup

**Lime syrup**

250 g (8 oz) sugar

250 ml (8 fl oz) water

juice and rind of 1 lime

lime segments, pith and pips
removed (optional)

**Licorice parfait**

300 ml (10 fl oz) cream

50 g (1½ oz) licorice

2 free-range eggs

1 egg yolk

2 tsp glucose

60 g (2 oz) sugar

2 tbsp Pernod

**For the lime syrup** Bring the sugar
and water to the boil, stirring to ensure
the sugar is dissolved. Remove from
heat and add the lime juice and the
rind to taste. Stir well and refrigerate.

**For the licorice parfait** In a small
saucepan combine the cream and
licorice and heat gently, without
boiling, until the licorice is very soft.
Blend the mixture in a food processor
until well combined and pour through
a fine sieve to strain out the tiny
pieces of licorice. Set aside to cool.

In a small saucepan inside a larger
saucepan of gently simmering water,
make a sabayon by whisking together
the eggs, yolk, glucose, sugar and
Pernod until the mixture turns pale
and fluffy. Remove from heat and
continue whisking until it cools a little.

Fold half of the sabayon into the
licorice mixture. Once combined, fold
in the remaining sabayon until well
combined. Pour into individual moulds,
or in 1 log-shaped tin, and freeze.

*Serves 6*

**To serve** *Lower the moulds into hot
water for a few seconds before turning
out the parfait. You can either pour over
the lime syrup, or serve it on the table
in a jug. Garnish with lime segments*

# Mascarpone Semifreddo

1 punnet strawberries

1 punnet blueberries

1 punnet raspberries

1 punnet blackberries

25 ml (¾ fl oz) balsamic vinegar

100 ml (3½ fl oz) sugar syrup
(see page 226)

6 sheets filo pastry

125 g (4 oz) butter, melted

50 g (1¾ oz) icing sugar

1 tbsp ground cinnamon

50 g (1¾ oz) pistachios, finely chopped

100 g (3½ oz) mascarpone

## Mascarpone semifreddo

50 ml (1⅔ fl oz) water

200 g (7 oz) caster sugar

3 eggs, separated

1 vanilla bean, split and seeds
scraped out

zest of 1 lemon

300 g (10½ oz) mascarpone,
at room temperature

75 ml (2½ fl oz) cream, semi-whipped

Hull and wash the berries. Mix the balsamic vinegar and sugar syrup together, reserve 2 tablespoons and pour the rest over the berries. Set aside.

**For the semifreddo** Put water and 150 g (5 oz) of the sugar in a heavy-based saucepan and heat to 116°C (234°F): this is the softball stage (to check, drop tiny amount of syrup in cold water: it should form a soft, pliable ball).

Whisk the egg yolks until pale then whisk syrup into egg yolk. Mix in the vanilla seeds and lemon zest. Beat the egg whites and remaining 50 g (1¾ oz) sugar until soft peaks form. Soften mascarpone by beating. In a bowl fold softened mascarpone into the egg-yolk mixture, when it is combined then fold in cream, followed by egg whites.

Line a tray about 25 cm x 14 cm (10 in x 5½ in) and about 1 cm (½ in) deep with baking paper. Spread mixture in tray and freeze overnight. Once frozen cut into 8 cm (3¼ in) squares.

Lay a sheet of filo on bench and brush it with melted butter. Dust with icing sugar and cinnamon and spread with nuts. Layer another sheet on top to make a sandwich. Repeat the process, making sandwiches until filo used up. Refrigerate for 1 hour then cut into 8 cm squares. Preheat oven to 180°C (350°F) and bake filo for 9 minutes or until golden.

Combine the 100 g (3½ oz) mascarpone with the reserved 2 tablespoons balsamic syrup.

*Serves 6*

**To serve** *Place a square of filo on each plate and top with the frozen mascarpone square. Place another square of filo on top, spoon over berries and mascarpone cream. Place another filo square with more berries and cream over that, then a final square of filo dusted with icing sugar. Drizzle the syrup from the berry mixture around the plate.*

# Vanilla Bavarois with Poached Rhubarb

**Vanilla bavarois**

3 egg yolks

2 tbsp caster sugar

2 tbsp brown sugar

2 leaves gelatine

500 ml (2 cups/1 pt) milk

3 vanilla beans, cut in half lengthwise

100 ml (3½ fl oz) cream

**Poached rhubarb**

4 stalks rhubarb

2 tbsp sugar syrup (see page 226)

lemon juice to taste

**To make bavarois** In a small bowl, whisk the egg yolks with the caster sugar and brown sugar until combined. Set aside. Place the gelatine leaves in cold water to soften.

Pour the milk into a small saucepan and add the vanilla beans. Bring to the boil. Remove from the heat and pour the hot milk and vanilla beans into the egg mixture. Gently whisk until combined, then pour the hot liquid back into the saucepan. Stir gently over a very low heat for a minute or two (do not boil or the mixture will separate), or until the mixture thickens very slightly to coat the back of a spoon. Remove from heat.

Squeeze excess water from the gelatine leaves and add them to the hot mixture, stirring gently for a minute or two, or until dissolved. Strain the liquid through a fine sieve into a bowl and sit it on ice to allow the mixture to cool and slightly thicken (5–10 minutes). Stir in the cream.

Pour the mixture into 6 ½-cup lightly oiled dariole moulds and set in the fridge overnight. To serve, sit the moulds in warm water for a few seconds to loosen the bavarois slightly, run a knife around the top, then upturn the wobbly custard onto plates. Serve with poached rhubarb.

**To make poached rhubarb** Chop rhubarb into 5 cm (2 in) long pieces. Coat with sugar syrup and a squeeze of lemon juice. Put in a saucepan, cover the fruit with a piece of greaseproof paper and cook over low heat until the rhubarb is slightly collapsed.

*Serves 6*

**To serve** *Place the rhubarb on a plate next to a bavarois with a little bit of poaching juice around the outside.*

# Strawberry Tartlets

100 g (3½ oz) sweet pastry
(see page 220)

**Purée**

1 punnet strawberries

1 tbsp caster sugar

30 ml (1 fl oz) strawberry liqueur

**Filling**

1 egg

4 egg yolks

60 ml (2 fl oz) water

30 ml (1 fl oz) glucose syrup

75 g (2⅔ oz) caster sugar

200 ml (7 fl oz) strawberry purée

150 ml (5 fl oz) cream

few extra strawberries, sliced

Preheat oven to 150°C (300°F). Grease tartlet moulds and line with sweet pastry (the number made will depend on the size of moulds). Prick pastry bases and cover them with greaseproof paper weighed down by a little rice in the middle. Bake for 6–10 minutes. Remove rice and paper, turn the oven up to 170°C (340°F) and cook until pastry is golden brown.

**To make purée** Clean and hull strawberries, then put in saucepan with sugar and liqueur. Wet a piece of greaseproof paper and put directly on top of strawberries, then cook on medium heat until they are soft. Allow to cool and process or blend until a purée. Measure 200 ml (7 fl oz) of purée and set aside.

**For filling** Beat egg and yolks in a mixer until they are light and fluffy. At the same time heat water, glucose and sugar together until syrup reaches a softball consistency. Slowly add glucose mix to eggs and beat until cool. Stir in the 200 ml (7 fl oz) of strawberry purée. Whip cream to soft peaks and fold into mix. Pipe filling into sweet pastry cases and freeze until set, approximately 2 hours. Serve with a slice of strawberry on top.

*Serves 6–10*

*Notes Strawberry purée is great to use in milkshakes and cocktails.*

*You can use any berry or liqueur of your choice in this recipe.*

*You can freeze any leftover filling.*

*If you don't have tartlet moulds you can use muffin trays.*

# Pancakes with Caramelised Bananas

**Pancakes**

150 g (5 oz) plain flour

1½ tbsp caster sugar

4 free-range eggs

150 ml (5 fl oz) milk

150 ml (5 fl oz) cream

oil to grease pan

**Caramelised bananas**

1 tbsp butter

6 bananas, peeled and halved vertically

6 tbsp icing sugar

**Topping**

100 ml (3½ fl oz) maple syrup

50 ml (1½ fl oz) cream

**For the pancakes** Sift the flour into a large bowl, add the sugar and make a well. Crack the eggs into the well, add the milk and cream and whisk the mixture until it is smooth. Leave to rest for 30 minutes.

Heat a little oil in a frying pan and ladle in some of the pancake batter. Cook over a low heat until golden brown, then flip over and cook the other side. Repeat until all the batter has been used (makes about 6 pancakes).

**Meanwhile, for the caramelised bananas** In another pan, melt the butter, add the bananas and sprinkle liberally with icing sugar. Cook over a medium heat on both sides, until the sugar caramelises.

**For the topping** Mix together the maple syrup and cream and pour into a jug.

*Serves 6*

*To serve* Place 2 banana pieces on each warm pancake and dust with icing sugar. Serve with the jug of maple cream.

# Stewed Strawberries with Yoghurt

*This dish also makes a lovely breakfast or lunchtime dessert.*

2 punnets strawberries

50 ml (1½ fl oz) water

200 g (6½ oz) sugar

2 vanilla beans, split lengthwise

300 g (10 oz) natural yoghurt

Put the washed, hulled strawberries, water and sugar in a saucepan. Scrape the vanilla seeds into the saucepan as well. Bring to the boil and then simmer for about 10 minutes, or until slightly reduced, stirring occasionally. Remove from heat and cool.

*Serves 4*

**To serve** *Spoon the strawberries and their juices into serving bowls and drop a generous dollop of yoghurt on top.*

# Fruit Plate with Ricotta & Honey

400 g (14 oz) fresh fruit
(e.g. mango, berries, apples, bananas, melon, stone fruits)

200 g (6½ oz) fresh ricotta

honey

Wash and cut the fruit into generous serving pieces.

*Serves 4*

**To serve** *Arrange on serving plates, spoon a mound of ricotta in the middle and drizzle with honey.*

# White Chocolate Truffles

500 g (1 lb) white chocolate

60 g (2 oz) butter

110 ml (3¾ fl oz) cream

70 ml (2½ fl oz) Baileys liqueur

400 g (14 oz) 66 per cent dark chocolate (see notes)

cocoa powder, to serve

Chop white chocolate up into little squares and put in bowl. Dice butter and add to chocolate.

Bring cream and Baileys to the boil together and pour this over chocolate, whisking until chocolate and butter have dissolved and the mixture – a ganache – is smooth. Strain, put in a container and leave in freezer for a few hours.

Gently melt 300 g (10 oz) of the dark chocolate in a pan over a bain marie and while it is melting chop remaining 100 g (4 oz). When chocolate is melted use a wooden spoon to stir chopped chocolate through. Let sit.

With a parisienne scoop (or melon baller) dipped in hot water scoop the ganache into balls and put back into freezer on a tray. When the balls are cold use hands to roll them into rounder, smoother shapes – work quickly so that the heat of your hands does not melt the mixture. Put back in the freezer to solidify once more.

Using a fork, dunk rolled ganache through the melted chocolate until coated, allow to solidify for a moment or two, then dust with cocoa powder. Refrigerate immediately. Store in fridge and serve with coffee after dinner.

*Notes* The quality of chocolate depends on the amount of cocoa solid it includes. Good quality converture chocolate will specify the percentage of cocoa solids it contains: try to find 66 per cent.

Use this recipe to make dark chocolate truffles instead of white – use only dark chocolate in the ingredients. You can also substitute different alcohols for the Baileys: rum and Grand Marnier are both delicious.

213

# Chocolate Panforte

100 g (3½ oz) dried figs, chopped

75 g (2½ oz) glacé ginger, finely chopped

100 g (3½ oz) mixed rind

200 g (6½ oz) hazelnuts

125 g (4 oz) macadamia nuts

225 g (7 oz) plain flour

4 tbsp cocoa

½ tsp ground cinnamon

½ tsp ground cloves

250 ml (8 fl oz) honey

200 g (6½ oz) caster sugar

125 g (4 oz) dark chocolate

icing sugar for dusting

Preheat the oven to 160ºC (325ºF). Line a 19 cm x 29 cm x 2 cm (8 in x 11 in x 1 in) cake tin or baking tray with baking paper.

In a large bowl, mix together all the ingredients except the honey, sugar and chocolate.

In a small saucepan bring the honey and sugar to the boil, then add the chocolate, stirring until melted. Pour the hot mixture into the dry ingredients and stir well. If it's too dry, add 1–2 tbsp water. The mixture should be very sticky. Stir well until thoroughly incorporated.

Press the mixture into the tin and bake for 1 hour, or until the top feels spongy to touch. Cool in the tin and turn out. Remove the baking paper.

*To serve* Cut the panforte into small squares, rectangles or diamonds and dust with icing sugar.

# Blueberry Friands

75 g (2½ oz) plain flour

240 g (7½ oz) icing sugar

125 g (4 oz) ground almonds

1 tbsp grated lemon rind

6 egg whites

180 g (6 oz) butter, melted

75 g (2½ oz) blueberries

Preheat the oven to 210°C (415°F). Grease friand tins, or you can use muffin tins (although friands are traditionally oval-shaped).

Sift the flour and icing sugar into a large bowl. Add the ground almonds and lemon rind and mix well.

Lightly beat the egg whites, so that they are white and frothy but not stiff like meringue. Stir them into the mixture, along with the melted butter. Carefully fold in the blueberries.

Spoon the mixture into the tins, to fill about two-thirds of the moulds. Bake for 15 minutes at 210°C (415°F), then turn the oven down to 200°C (400°F) and bake for a further 10 minutes.

Allow friands to cool in the tins for 5 minutes, then turn out on a wire rack.

*Makes 10–12*

# Vanilla Bean Shortbread

140 g (4½ oz) butter

60 g (2 oz) caster sugar

225 g (7 oz) plain flour

1 free-range egg yolk

½ vanilla bean, seeds only

½ tsp vanilla essence

Cream the butter and sugar. Mix in the flour, then the yolk, vanilla bean seeds and vanilla essence. Bring the dough together with your hands then divide it in half. On 2 sheets of baking paper, roll each portion of dough into a cylinder shape, about 4 cm (1½ in) diameter. Place the 2 rolls in the fridge until they harden a little (about 45 minutes).

Preheat the oven to 160°C (325°F). Remove the paper and cut the rolls into rounds about 1 cm (½ in) thick. Place on baking paper laid over baking trays and cook for 10–12 minutes, or until they are just turning golden brown.

*Makes about 30 biscuits*

# Almond Honey Slice

250 g (8 oz) butter

150 g (5 oz) caster sugar

100 ml (3½ fl oz) honey

75 ml (2½ fl oz) cream

75 ml (2½ fl oz) brandy

300 g (10 oz) flaked almonds

150 g (5 oz) unsalted
pistachio nuts, shelled

200 g (6½ oz) dark or milk chocolate

Preheat the oven to 200°C (400°F). Line the base and sides of a 19 cm x 29 cm (8 in x 11 in) lamington tin with baking paper.

In a medium saucepan, melt the butter, add the sugar, honey, cream and brandy. Bring to the boil, remove from heat and add the nuts. Mix well.

Spread into the tin and cook for 25–30 minutes, or until the top goes golden brown. Remove and cool.

Once cool, melt the chocolate in a small saucepan inside a larger saucepan of gently simmering water. Drizzle the chocolate over the top of the slice, or spread the chocolate with a knife to cover. Refrigerate.

**To serve** *When the slice is cold, cut into squares and refrigerate until ready to eat.*

# Orange Lamingtons

**Sponge**

8 eggs, separated

extra 2 egg yolks

190 g (7½ oz) caster sugar

80 g (2¾ oz) plain flour

40 g (1⅓ oz) cornflour

grated zest of 1 orange

40 g (2 tbsp) butter, melted and cooled

**Icing**

30 g (1 oz) butter

125 ml ½ cup) boiling water

300 g (2½ cups) icing sugar, sifted

3 tbsp orange jelly crystals

juice of 1 orange

100 g (1½ cups) desiccated coconut

Preheat the oven to 180°C (350°F).

**To make the sponge** Beat the 10 yolks with 90 g (3 oz) of the sugar until very pale (5–10 minutes). Transfer to a large bowl. Sift the flour and cornflour three times, then fold into the yolk mixture. Add zest to yolk mixture.

Beat the egg whites with the remaining 100 g (3½ oz) sugar until stiff and glossy. Fold three-quarters of the whites into the yolk mixture. Mix the melted butter with the remaining whites until well combined, then fold into the yolk mixture.

Pour into a greased lamington tin (measuring about 31 cm x 25 cm x 3 cm/12½ in x 10 in x 1 in) lined with greaseproof paper. Bake for 12–15 minutes, or until golden brown and spongy to touch. Turn the sponge out on a wire rack and cover with a tea towel to cool.

**To make the icing** Melt the butter in the boiling water. Pour it over the icing sugar and jelly crystals and stir until dissolved. Stir in the orange juice.

Cut the sponge into 6 cm x 6 cm (2 in x 2 in) squares. Dip them in the orange jelly liquid and roll in coconut.

*Makes 20*

*Notes Make a big, traditional sponge cake by baking two identical cakes (using the sponge recipe for the lamingtons). Place one on top of the other, joined by a layer of jam and sweetened whipped cream. Spread more whipped cream on top, spread jam on the sides and sprinkle the whole cake with coconut. Top with fresh fruit, such as strawberries, kiwifruit, blueberries, raspberries, passionfruit or sliced stone fruit.*

*You can use any flavour of jelly crystals.*

# Basics

# Sweet Pastry

250 g (8 oz) plain flour

90 g (3 oz) icing sugar

125 g (4 oz) butter, cubed

½ vanilla bean, split vertically, seeds only

1 free-range egg

Sieve the flour and icing sugar into a large bowl. Gradually add the cubes of butter and rub them in with your fingers. (You can use a food processor to combine until it resembles breadcrumbs.)

Make a well in the centre, and add the vanilla seeds. Beat the egg and pour into the well. Stir a little with a wooden spoon, then use your hands to mix well until it all comes together in one ball. If it's too dry, add a little water.

Wrap it in clingfilm and refrigerate for 30 minutes before rolling out.

*Makes enough for 1 large tart*

# Savoury Pastry

350 g (11½ oz) plain flour

pinch of sea salt

150 g (5 oz) butter, cubed

2 free-range eggs

125 ml (4 fl oz) water

Sieve the flour and salt into a large bowl. Gradually add the cubes of butter and rub them in with your fingers. (You can use a food processor to combine until it resembles breadcrumbs.)

Make a well in the centre. Beat the eggs and add to the well, then the cold water and stir a little until well combined. Use your hands to bring the mixture together to form a dough, adding a little extra flour if it is too sticky.

Wrap in clingfilm and refrigerate for 30 minutes before rolling out.

*Makes enough for 2 large tarts*

# Fish Stock

1.5 kg (3 lb) fish bones

2 onions, finely chopped

2 celery stalks, finely chopped

2 leeks, white part only, finely sliced

1 clove garlic, crushed

Chop the fish bones with a cleaver or a heavy knife (you will fit more in the pot). Rinse the bones under cold water until the water runs clear. Place bones in a large pot, cover with water and bring to the boil. Add the onion, celery, leeks and garlic. Simmer for 20 minutes, skimming any froth off the top as you go. Strain, cool, cover and then refrigerate.

*Makes about 2 litres (3¼ pt)*

# Chicken Stock

2 kg (4 lb) chicken bones, chopped roughly

2 celery stalks, finely chopped

2 leeks, white part only, finely sliced

3 onions, finely chopped

1 clove garlic, crushed

Place the chicken bones in a very large pot (you may need two), cover with cold water and bring to the boil. Skim any froth from the surface. Add the celery, leeks, onions and garlic and simmer for 2 hours, skimming the top every now and then, and topping up with cold water to keep the bones mainly covered. Strain, cool, cover and refrigerate until ready to use.

*Makes about 3 litres (5 pt)*

# Duck Stock

Follow the recipe for Chicken Stock, above, but use roasted duck bones or duck carcass.

# Beef Stock

3 kg (6 lb) beef bones

2 celery stalks, roughly chopped

2 onions, roughly chopped

1 carrot, roughly chopped

2 tbsp tomato paste

375 ml (1½ cups) red wine

4 stalks flat-leaf parsley

2 bay leaves

Preheat oven to 200°C (400°F). Place chopped beef bones in a baking dish and bake for 30 minutes or until golden brown. Put the beef bones in a large stockpot, cover with water and bring to the boil.

Put the vegetables in another baking tray and bake until golden (about 20 minutes), take out of oven and mix in tomato paste, put back into the oven for 5 minutes to cook the tomato paste.

Add vegetables to the beef bones. Deglaze the vegetable pan with the wine (let wine bubble in pan and scrape any burnt bits into the liquid, to dissolve) and add to the bones with the parsley and bay. Allow the stock to slowly but constantly simmer. Occasionally skim the surface of the stock while it is cooking, so the stock remains clear.

Simmer the stock for 4–6 hours, topping the stock up with a little cold water occasionally to keep the bones mainly covered (the longer the cooking time the better the flavour will be).

*Makes 5–6 litres (10–12 pt)*

# Veal Stock

Follow the recipe for Beef Stock, above, but use veal bones instead of beef bones.

# Clarified Butter

250 g (8 oz) unsalted butter

Melt the butter over a very gentle heat and slowly bring to the boil. Skim all the white froth from the surface. Remove from heat and slowly pour the butter into a bowl, being careful not to pour in any of the white sediment on the bottom of the pan. The clarified butter should be of a similar consistency to extra-virgin olive oil and will keep in the fridge for several weeks.

*Makes about 200 g (6½ oz) (clarified butter loses about 20 per cent of its original weight)*

# Preserved Lemon

6 lemons

100 ml (3 fl oz) lemon juice

100 ml (3 fl oz) white wine vinegar

1 packet Maldon sea salt

100 ml (3 fl oz) extra-virgin olive oil

3 cinnamon sticks

3 star anise

2 bay leaves

Steam lemons for 7 minutes to soften. Quarter and squeeze juice into a bowl. Pack lemons with sea salt. Place in a sterilised jar, leave for 1 hour. Pour lemon juice, vinegar, olive oil and the spices over the lemon quarters and seal. Store in a dark cool place. Invert on a daily basis.

This is best if made a week before use and the lemons will last for up to 1 month. Refrigerate jar once opened.

# Pickled Ginger

350 g (12⅓ oz) ginger, peeled

250 ml (1 cup) sugar syrup
(see page 226)

Using a sharp knife thinly slice the
ginger. Blanch in boiling water three
times, each time refreshing in icy cold
water. Boil sugar syrup and pour over
blanched ginger. Store in a sterilised jar.

*Notes* *This will last forever in the jar
– but do make sure the jar is sterilised.*

*When you've used the ginger,
keep the syrup: you can use it in
cooking or to pickle more ginger.*

# Hollandaise Sauce

4 free-range egg yolks

100 ml (3½ fl oz) tarragon
vinegar

50 ml (1½ fl oz) dry white wine

500 ml (1 pint) clarified
butter (see page 223)

sea salt and freshly ground
black pepper

In a small saucepan inside a larger
saucepan of gently simmering water,
whisk the egg yolks, vinegar and
white wine until thickened and
creamy (about 4 minutes). Remove
from heat and slowly pour in clarified
butter, whisking continuously,
until well combined. Season.

*Makes about 500 ml (1 pint)*

# Mayonnaise

2 free-range egg yolks

2 tsp Dijon mustard

2 tsp white wine vinegar

200 ml (6½ fl oz) extra-virgin olive oil

sea salt and freshly ground pepper

In a small bowl, whisk (or use an
electric beater) the yolks, mustard and
vinegar until well combined. Slowly
drizzle in the extra-virgin olive oil,
whisking or beating continuously,
until well emulsified. Season.

If the mayonnaise is too thick, thin
it down with a little hot water.

*Makes 250 ml*

# Onion Confit

100 g (3½ oz) butter

2 brown onions, peeled and finely sliced

100 ml (3½ fl oz) honey

100 ml (3½ fl oz) dry white wine

50 ml (1½ fl oz) sherry
or balsamic vinegar

sea salt and freshly ground
black pepper

Melt the butter in a heavy-bottomed saucepan. Add the onions and cook over very low heat for 10 minutes. Add the honey and wine and cook over a very low heat for about 45 minutes. Add the sherry vinegar and season to taste.

*Makes about 250 g (8 oz)*

# Sugar Syrup

500 g (1 lb) white sugar

500 ml (2 cups) cold water

Put sugar and water in a saucepan and boil until sugar dissolves.

*Makes 1 litre (1⅔ pt)*

**Note** *Sugar syrup lasts for a long time and is handy to have made up. Store in a sterilised jar in the refrigerator.*

# Index

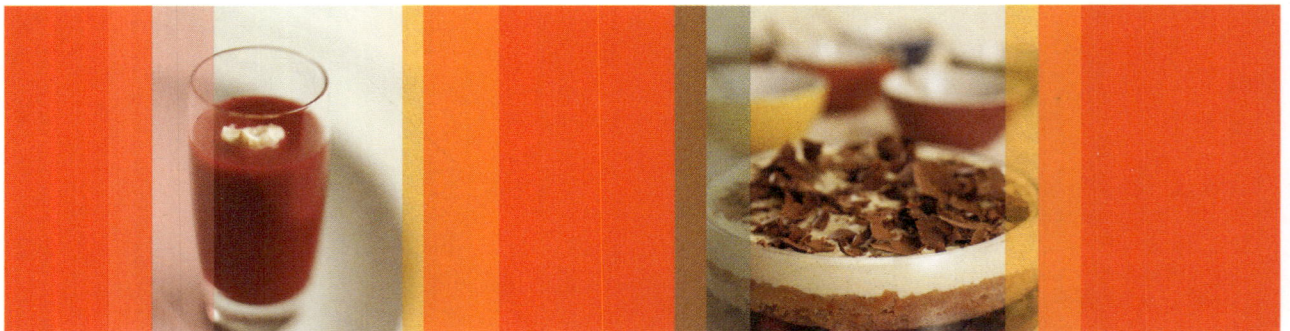